MW01109085

# Norton Utilities™ 5
# Instant Reference

*Michael Gross*

SYBEX®

San Francisco • Paris • Düsseldorf • Soest

Acquisitions Editor: Dianne King
Series Editor: James A. Compton
Editor: Richard Mills
Technical Editor: Nick Dargahi
Word Processors: Scott Campbell, Ann Dunn, Lisa Mitchell
Series Book Designer: Ingrid Owen
Production Artist: Eleanor Ramos
Screen Graphics: Cuong Le
Desktop Publishing Production: Len Gilbert
Proofreader/Production Assistant: Patsy Owens
Indexer: Nancy Anderman Guenther
Cover Designer: Archer Design
Screen reproductions produced by XenoFont.

XenoFont is a trademark of XenoSoft.

SYBEX is a registered trademark of SYBEX, Inc.

TRADEMARKS: SYBEX has attempted throughout this book to distinguish proprietary trademarks from descriptive terms by following the capitalization style used by the manufacturer.

SYBEX is not affiliated with any manufacturer.

Every effort has been made to supply complete and accurate information. However, SYBEX assumes no responsibility for its use, nor for any infringement of the intellectual property rights of third parties which would result from such use.

The text of this book is printed on recycled paper.

Copyright ©1991 SYBEX Inc., 2021 Challenger Drive, Alameda, CA 94501. World rights reserved. No part of this publication may be stored in a retrieval system, transmitted, or reproduced in any way, including but not limited to photocopy, photograph, magnetic or other record, without the prior agreement and written permission of the publisher.

Library of Congress Card Number: TK 90-71330
ISBN: 0-89588-737-1
Manufactured in the United States of America
10 9 8 7 6 5 4 3 2 1

# SYBEX INSTANT REFERENCES

We've designed SYBEX *Instant References* to meet the evolving needs of software users, who want essential information easily accessible, in a clear and concise form. Our best authors have distilled their expertise into compact reference guides in which you can look up the precise steps for using any feature, including the available options. More than just summaries, these books also provide insights into effective usage drawn from our authors' wealth of experience.

Other SYBEX *Instant References* are:

*AutoCAD Instant Reference*
George Omura

*dBASE IV 1.1 Programmer's
Instant Reference*
Alan Simpsor

*dBASE IV 1.1 User's
Instant Reference*
Alan Simpson

*DOS Instant Reference*
Greg Harvey and
Kay Yarborough Nelson

*Harvard Graphics Instant
Reference* (December 1990)
Gerald Jones

*Lotus 1-2-3 Instant Reference,
Release 2.2*
Greg Harvey and
Kay Yarborough Nelson

*PC Tools Deluxe 6 Instant Reference*
Gordon McComb

*Windows 3.0  Instant Reference*
(December 1990)
Marshall L. Moseley

*WordPerfect 5 Instant Reference*
Greg Harvey and
Kay Yarborough Nelson

*WordPerfect 5.1 Instant Reference*
Greg Harvey and
Kay Yarborough Nelson

*This book is dedicated to the memory of my uncle, Irving Judson*

*1911–1990*

# *Acknowledgments*

There are a great many people who contributed significantly to this book and thanks are due all of them. If I have missed anyone, I assure you it was unintentional and I offer my apologies in advance.

- To Dianne King, acquisitions editor, for rolling the dice a little bit and giving me the opportunity.

- To Jim Compton, series editor, whose help was invaluable in deciding issues of structure and content.

- To Richard Mills, editor, who wielded his peculiar glamour on my too often discursive prose and who belies the myth that editors are difficult and unpleasant to work with.

- To Nick Dargahi, technical editor, who made sure I got it all right and explained it all clearly.

- To the word processors (alphabetically), Scott Campbell, Ann Dunn, and Lisa Mitchell, for building the manuscript and for putting up with some inconvenient changes.

- To the members of Production (in no particular order), who made the physical thing: Len Gilbert and Dan Brodnitz, typesetters; Patsy Owens, proofreader and production assistant; Eleanor Ramos, artist; and Cuong Le, conjuror of screens.

- To Ingrid Owen, series designer, for making the thing look sexy.

- To Brendan Fletcher and Janna Hecker, assistant editors, who did just enough to get mentioned.

- To the members of the Tech Department, and to Dave Clark, member emeritus, for their support and good humor.

- To my mother, Katherine, my father, Leonard, and my sister, Rachel, and to all of my extended family, for their love and encouragement.

- And finally, thanks are due to Linda, for everything.

# Table of Contents

Introduction                            ix

BE                                        1
  ASK                                     1
  BEEP                                    2
  BOX                                     3
  CLS                                     3
  DELAY                                   4
  GOTO                                    4
  PRINTCHAR                               4
  ROWCOL                                  5
  SA                                      5
  WINDOW                                  6

CALIBRAT                                  7

DISKEDIT                                 11
  Edit/Object Functions                  11
  Window Functions                       25
  Info Functions                         29
  Tools Functions                        30
  Quit Functions                         35

DISKMON                                  37

DISKREET                                 41

DISKTOOL                                 55

FILEFIND                                 61

FILEFIX                                  71

FILESAVE                                          77

IMAGE                                             81

NCACHE-F, NCACHE-S                                83

NCC                                              87

NCD                                              95

NDD                                              99

NORTON                                          105

SFORMAT                                         113

SPEEDISK                                        117

SYSINFO                                         127

UNERASE                                         133

UNFORMAT                                        145

WIPEINFO                                        147


Appendix: Installing the Norton Utilities        153
  Installing the Program                         153
  Modifying Your CONFIG.SYS File Manually        157


Index                                           158

# *Introduction*

The intent of this book is simple. It is designed to help users of the Norton Utilities version 5.0 find information about the package quickly and easily. It will be the most helpful to users who have some familiarity with the software and need information on something in particular that is eluding them or want to try out aspects of a program unfamiliar to them. PC users who are new to the package will also find the book sufficient to give them a working knowledge of the programs.

## HOW THIS BOOK IS ORGANIZED

There is one section devoted to each of the programs that comprise the package. Within each section you will find a summary description of the program and its capabilities, upgrade information relating the program to its predecessors in version 4.5, if any, an annotated sequence of steps detailing each of the program's functions, and complete command-line syntax. The sections are ordered alphabetically, as are the program functions within each section (with the exception of DISKEDIT where, due to the size of the program, functions are grouped first by type and then alphabetically within each type).

## NAVIGATING THE INTERFACE

All but three of the programs in the Norton Utilities 5.0 (BE, IMAGE, and NCACHE) have an interactive interface, replete with pull-down menus, dialog boxes, lists, and options of various sorts. For the sake of economy and clarity, the sequences of steps throughout the book only tell you to "select" this or that option. What "select" means in any particular case depends entirely upon what you are selecting where. The following sections detail the different parts of the interactive interface and how to navigate each of them.

## Using Pull-down Menus

You can pull down a menu in one of three ways:

- Press the Alt key alone or F10. This pulls down the first menu on the left of the menu bar. You can then access the +menu you want by pressing ← and → as needed.

- Hold down the Alt key and press the first letter of the menu's name—to pull down the File menu, for example, hold down the Alt key and press F.

- Place the mouse pointer on the menu name and click the left button.

Once the menu you want is pulled down, there are four ways to select an option:

- Use ↑ and ↓ to highlight the option, and press ↵.

- Press the highlighted letter in the option's name (represented in this book in a lighter face).

- Place the mouse pointer on the option and click the left button.

- Press the Ctrl or Alt key combination listed next to the option. Such a combination is not available for all options.

## Using List Boxes

Often you will be required to select an item from a list of items within a box (usually files, directories, or drives). If the list contains more items than can be displayed at once, you can display different parts of the list as follows:

- Press ↑ and ↓ as needed.

- Press the Home key to go to the beginning of the list.

- Press the End key to go to the end of the list.

- Place the mouse pointer on the scroll box (the solid rectangular block) on the scroll bar, which comprises the right-hand edge of the list box. Click the left button and hold it down. Drag the box up or down as needed and release the button when you're finished.

You can select an item from a list in one of the following ways:

- Highlight the item with a combination of ↑, ↓, Home, and End, and press ↵ or select the accompanying OK option.

- Place the mouse pointer on the item, and double-click the left button or click the right button once.

- Place the mouse pointer on the item, click the left button once, and then select the accompanying OK option.

## Using Dialog Box Menus

A dialog box menu is the list of options, each of which is a small rectangle, that usually appears horizontally across the bottom of a dialog box or vertically down the left, though there are other configurations. You can select an option in one of the following ways:

- Use the cursor keys to highlight an option and press ↵.

- Press the capitalized letter of the option.

- Move the mouse pointer to the option and click the left button.

## Using Toggle Options and Radio Buttons

A *toggle option* appears as a box in graphics mode or as square brackets in text mode. When activated, it is marked with a check mark in graphics mode and with an *x* in text mode. A *radio button* appears as a circle in graphics mode or as parentheses in text mode. When activated, it is marked with a filled circle (larger in graphics mode than in text mode).

When you activate one radio button, it automatically turns off the others in the group. Toggle options are independent of one another and can be turned on or off regardless of the state of neighboring toggle options.

You can turn toggle options and buttons on or off in either of the following ways:

- Use ↑, ↓, ←, or → to move the cursor to the option and press the spacebar. The spacebar also cycles you through a group of buttons.

- Move the mouse pointer to the option and click the left button.

## Using Prompts

Prompts are those sections of a dialog box where you are required to enter text. The standard editing keys are available when typing text at a prompt:

- The Home key moves you to the beginning of the line, and the End key moves you to the end.

- The ← and → keys move the cursor one space to the left and right, respectively.

- The Backspace key deletes the character to the left of the cursor. The Delete key deletes the character at the cursor position.

To move the cursor with the mouse, position the mouse pointer at the new location and click the left button.

## Navigating within Dialog Boxes

Dialog boxes are often crowded with many different kinds of options; similar options tend to be grouped together. You can move among these discrete groups in the following ways:

- Press the Tab key to move from one group to the next—for example, from a prompt to the first button in a buttons area to the first option on a dialog box menu.

- Press one of the arrow keys to move to the next option, regardless of the group.

- Move the mouse pointer to the option you want. (Click the left button to select the option.)

The mouse is the most efficient means of selecting an option. If, however, you do not have a mouse or simply prefer the keyboard, some combination of the Tab key and the arrow keys works best.

# GETTING HELP

Help is available for each of the programs that constitute the Norton Utilities 5.0. To get help on a topic, follow these steps:

**1.** Click the left mouse button on **F1=Help** in the upper-right corner of the screen, or press **F1**.

**2.** In the Help dialog box, highlight a topic and select **Help**. You can select **Cancel** at this point to return to the program.

**3.** When you've finished reading, select **Cancel** to return to the program. Alternatively, select **Next** to see help on the next topic in the list, select **Previous** to see help on the previous topic, or select **Topics** to go back to the list of topics. Selecting Topics returns you to step 2.

Help is context-sensitive—that is, if you are in the middle of an operation or a sequence of steps, selecting Help takes you directly to the description of that function.

The sequence of steps above requires that the program you are working in has an interactive mode (interactive help, therefore, is unavailable in BE, IMAGE, and NCACHE, which are command-line programs only). Command-line help is available for these and all other programs: Simply enter the program name, followed by a ?, at the command line, and press ↵. You will see a listing of command-line syntax and options.

# BE

## *The Batch Enhancer*

BE allows you to add the following enhancements to your batch files: custom menus or prompts, sound, boxes, windows, timed delays, color, branching, and cursor control.

● **UPGRADE INFORMATION**    Unlike many of the other programs in version 5.0, BE lacks an interactive mode and remains largely unchanged from version 4.5.

● **SYNTAX**

   **BE** *datafile*

or

   **BE** *command*

   ***datafile*** is the name of a file containing a list of BE commands. Each command must be on its own line, and the last line must end with a carriage return. Commands listed in *datafile* are not prefaced with BE as they are when executed from the command line or from a batch file. Commands within *datafile* can be grouped into subroutines marked off by a label and executed selectively. (See "GOTO.")

   ***command*** is one of ten possible BE commands, each having its own options and switches. Descriptions of these commands follow.

## ASK

Puts custom menus or prompts in batch files.

### Syntax

   **BE ASK** "*prompt*", (*keys*) (default=*key*) (timeout=*secs*) (adjust=*#*) (*color*) *"**prompt**"* is the text of the menu or prompt to be displayed. *Prompt* must be enclosed in quotation marks.

**keys** are the keys that are valid responses to *prompt*. Pressing a key other than the one listed causes a warning beep to sound. ASK provides conditional branching by returning a different DOS ERRORLEVEL code for each key in *keys*. The first key returns ERRORLEVEL 1, the second ERRORLEVEL 2, etc.

**default=***key* specifies the default choice.

**timeout=***secs* specifies the number of seconds ASK waits before automatically assuming the default. If no timeout is specified, ASK will wait forever.

**adjust=***#* adds a specified number (integer) to the DOS ERRORLEVEL code returned by each key in *keys*. ASK provides conditional branching by returning a different DOS ERRORLEVEL code for each key in *keys*. The first key returns the code ERRORLEVEL 1, the second ERRORLEVEL 2, etc. If, then, one of the menu choices calls up another menu, its first key will also return ERRORLEVEL 1 and its second key ERRORLEVEL 2. To prevent a conflict, use adjust=# to change the value of the ERRORLEVEL codes returned by one of the two menus. The maximum value for # is 254.

**color** specifies the color of the prompt. Valid colors are black, blue, green, cyan, red, magenta, yellow, white, gray, bright blue, bright green, bright cyan, bright red, bright magenta, bright yellow, and bright white. The *color* switch must be used in combination with some other optional switch.

## BEEP

Plays tones for a specified duration and of a specified pitch. Tones can be specified on the command line or grouped together in a file.

### Syntax

**BE BEEP (/D#) (/F#) (/R#) (/W#)**

or

**BE BEEP** *filename* **(/E)**

**/D**# specifies the duration of a tone in eighteenths of a second; # must be positive.

**/F**# specifies the frequency of a tone in hertz; # must be positive.

**/R**# specifies the number of times a tone is repeated; # must be positive.

**/W**# specifies the interval between tones in eighteenths of a second; # must be positive.

**filename** specifies the name of a file containing tones to be played. Tones are specified in *filename* just as they are on the command line by using the switches listed above.

**/E** echoes comments in *filename* to the screen. Comments are set off from commands by a semicolon. To be echoed, they must be enclosed in quotation marks (for example, /f440; "Middle C").

# BOX

Draws a box at specified screen coordinates.

## Syntax

**BE BOX** *TLCrow TLCcol BRCrow BRCcol* **(Single ¦ Double)** **(***color***)**

**TLCrow TLCcol** are the screen coordinates of the top-left corner of the box. *TLCrow* is the row in which this corner sits, and *TLCcol* is the column.

**BRCrow BRCcol** are the screen coordinates of the bottom-right corner of the box. *BRCrow* is the row in which this corner sits, and *BRCcol* is the column.

**Single ¦ Double** specifies whether the box is drawn with single or double lines.

**color** specifies the color of the box. Valid colors are the same as for the ASK prompt.

# CLS

Clears the screen.

## Syntax

**BE CLS**

# DELAY

Pauses batch-file execution for a specified length of time.

## Syntax

**BE DELAY #**

*#* specifies the duration of the pause in eighteenths of a second; # must be positive.

# GOTO

Allows for selective execution of BE commands within *datafile*. BE essentially supports the DOS GOTO batch file command, but within BE *datafiles*. See your DOS manual for more details.

## Syntax

**BE *datafile* ((GOTO)*label*)**

*datafile* is the file containing BE commands.

*label* is the name of the label within *datafile* marking the group of commands you want to execute. Labels in *datafile* are functionally identical to labels in DOS batch files.

# PRINTCHAR

Writes a character to the screen a specified number of times.

## Syntax

**BE PRINTCHAR *char* # (*color*)**

*char* is the character to be written.

*#* specifies the number of times the character is to be written.

*color* specifies the color of the character. Valid colors are the same as for the ASK prompt.

# ROWCOL

Positions the cursor and optionally writes text at specified screen coordinates.

## Syntax

**BE ROWCOL** *row col* **(***text***) (***color***)**

*row* is the row in which the cursor is positioned.

*col* is the column in which the cursor is positioned.

*text* is the text to be written at the new cursor position.

*color* specifies the color of the text. Valid colors are the same as for the ASK prompt.

# SA

The Screen Attributes command. Sets text, background, and border colors. For SA to be used, the ANSI.SYS driver must be loaded.

## Syntax

**BE SA** *default* **(/N) (/CLS)**

or

**BE SA (***intensity***) (***textcolor***) (ON** *background***) (/N) (/CLS)**

*default* manipulates the default display colors (white on black). The three valid settings are Normal, Reverse, and Underline.

*intensity* specifies the intensity of the foreground text. Can be set to Bright or Blinking.

*textcolor* specifies the color of the foreground text. Valid colors are black, blue, green, cyan, red, magenta, yellow, and white.

*background* specifies the background color. Valid colors are the same as for *textcolor*.

**/N** leaves the border color unchanged. (Normally, the border color is automatically set to the background color.) Use this switch to change the background color but not the border color.

**/CLS** clears the screen after colors are changed.

# WINDOW

Draws a window at specified screen coordinates.

## Syntax

**BE WINDOW** *TLCrow TLCcol BRCrow BRCcol* **(explode) (shadow) (color)**

*TLCrow TLCcol* are the screen coordinates (row and column) of the top-left corner of the window.

*BRCrow BRCcol* are the screen coordinates (row and column) of the bottom-right corner of the window.

**explode** causes the window to expand from its center to its final position when it is drawn.

**shadow** gives the window a three-dimensional look by drawing a shadow along the right and bottom edges of the window. The shadow does not obscure text underneath it.

*color* specifies the color of the window. Valid colors are the same as for the ASK prompt.

# CALIBRAT

CALIBRAT optimizes the performance of your hard disk by checking and optionally changing your hard-disk interleave and by testing
the integrity of every byte on the disk. Optimizing the interleave
maximizes the speed at which data is read from and written to your
hard disk. Checking every byte ensures the integrity of your data
by moving data from questionable or corrupted areas on the disk to
safe areas.

● **UPGRADE INFORMATION**   CALIBRAT is new to version
5.0 and has no predecessor in version 4.5.

## To Use the Disk Calibrator

1.  After starting CALIBRAT, an introductory screen appears.
    Select **Continue** when you are finished reading.

2.  Select a target drive. (This step is omitted if you have only
    one logical drive or if the drive is specified on the com-
    mand line.)

3.  You will see two information screens. Select **Continue**
    when you are finished reading them.

4.  After System Integrity Testing and Seek Testing, select
    **Continue**.

5.  After Data Encoding Testing, select **Continue**.

6.  Select an interleave.

7.  Select a level for Pattern Testing.

In step 4, **System Integrity Testing** checks to make sure that various
components and functions integral to the working of your hard disk
do, in fact, work properly. The computer's RAM, the hard-disk controller, the hard-disk controller's RAM, and the FATs (file allocation
tables) are checked, among others. CALIBRAT cannot correct any
errors it finds in these tests.

**Seek Testing** tests various aspects of the performance of your hard-
disk. **BIOS Seek Overhead** measures how long it takes for the

relevant ROM BIOS instructions to be executed when the hard disk is accessed. **Track-to-Track** measures how long it takes for the disk heads to move from one track to the next. **Full Stroke** measures how long it takes for the disk heads to move from the first track to the last. **Average Seek** measures how long it takes, on average, for the heads to find a randomly selected track. This is the most common measure of hard-disk speed.

In step 5, **Data Encoding Testing** checks your hard disk and hard-disk controller to determine the method by which data is written to the hard disk. Results are displayed in the Encoding Test box.

In step 6, you select an *interleave;* for "bookkeeping" purposes, DOS numbers each sector on a hard disk. When consecutively numbered sectors are located next to one another on your disk, the disk has a 1:1 interleave; when they are located every other sector, the disk has a 2:1 interleave; when they are located every third sector, the disk has a 3:1 interleave; and so on.

CALIBRAT determines your current interleave and checks other possible settings to determine which will allow your computer to read and write data the fastest. This setting, at which your hard disk makes the fewest revolutions when reading or writing some given amount of data, is said to be the *optimum interleave.*

CALIBRAT can alter the interleave of your hard disk by doing a nondestructive low-level format. This format, executed during Pattern Testing, is different from the format you normally do to prepare a disk for use and does not destroy any of your data.

In step 7, **Pattern Testing** checks every sector on your hard disk to make sure data can be written to it and read from it accurately. CALIBRAT writes and reads patterns of bits (0's and 1's)—if it finds an error in any byte, it marks the cluster containing that byte as bad, thus removing it from use by DOS. If there are any data on that cluster, they are moved to an errorless cluster.

Pattern Testing can take a number of hours, depending on the level you choose. It can be safely interrupted at any time by pressing **Esc** or by clicking either mouse button and can be resumed in a later session.

## • SYNTAX

### CALIBRAT (*drive*:) (/*options*)

*drive*: specifies the drive you want to calibrate.

The options are the following:

/**BATCH** omits introductory screens, information screens, and "Continue" prompts. It runs all tests consecutively and exits to DOS when finished.

/**BLANK** turns off the display during Pattern Testing.

/**NOCOPY** omits track copying during Pattern Testing.

/**NOFORMAT** omits the nondestructive low-level format (i.e., testing and changing the interleave).

/**NOSEEK** omits Seek Testing.

/**PATTERN:***n* sets the Pattern Testing level; *n* can be 0, 5, 40, or 80.

/**R:***filename* writes CALIBRAT's report to *filename*. If you use this switch, you must also use /BATCH.

/**RA:***filename* appends CALIBRAT's report to *filename*. If you use this switch, you must also use /BATCH.

/**X:***drives* excludes drives you specify from any testing. For Zenith DOS users only.

• **NOTES**    CALIBRAT cannot do a low-level format (adjust the interleave) on the following:

- Hard disks with SCSI or IDE controllers. The kind of controller you have is shown in Data Encoding Testing.
- Hard-disk controllers that use *sector translation;* that is, controllers that cause DOS to think that the number of sectors per track is different from what it actually is.
- Hard-disk controllers that have built-in disk caches.

CALIBRAT does not work on the following:

- Floppy drives
- Network drives or volumes
- RAM disks

- Drives created with the ASSIGN and SUBST commands in DOS
- Bernoulli boxes
- Novell file servers
- Hard disks with sectors larger than 512K

# DISKEDIT

DISKEDIT is perhaps the most powerful program in the Norton Utilities 5.0. Essentially a data editor, it allows you to edit (or simply view) any part of a disk. You can access data in files, directories, boot records, file allocation tables, partition tables, and in unused space. Be careful when you use DISKEDIT, as it is possible to damage files or drives, sometimes irrevocably.

● **UPGRADE INFORMATION** DISKEDIT incorporates the functions of three programs from version 4.5: NU (Norton Utility), FA (File Attributes), and FD (File Date and Time). NU, however, has been split into two programs for version 5.0. Its data-editing functions are found in DISKEDIT, and its file-unerasing functions are found in UNERASE.

## EDIT/OBJECT FUNCTIONS

### To Copy Marked Data

1. Mark data as a block (see "To Mark Data").
2. Pull down the Edit menu and select the C**opy** option, or press **Ctrl-C**.
3. Move to the area where the data is to be copied.
4. Pull down the Edit menu and select the P**aste Over** option, or press **Ctrl-V**.
5. Save your changes to disk: Pull down the Edit menu and select the W**rite changes** option, or press **Ctrl-W**.
6. Select **Write** in the Write Changes dialog box to confirm saving your changes to disk, or select **Review** to review your changes (this takes you back to where you were after step 4).

When you issue the Copy command, a copy of the marked data is placed in the clipboard. The Paste Over command then copies the data in the clipboard to the current cursor location. Once placed in the clipboard, data remains there until it is replaced (by copying another marked block). You can, therefore, paste the same data any number of times in different locations.

## To Edit the Boot Record

**Warning**: Since the boot record contains critical disk information, it is recommended that you do not make any changes to it.

1. Pull down the Object menu and select the **Boot record** option, or press **Alt-B**.
2. Make your changes.
3. Save your changes to disk: Pull down the Edit menu and select the **Write changes** option, or press **Ctrl-W**.
4. Select **Write** in the Write Changes dialog box to confirm saving your changes to disk, or select **Review** to review your changes (this takes you back to step 2).

The boot record contains both booting instructions and information about the physical layout of a disk, such as the version of DOS under which the disk was formatted, the number of sectors on the disk, and the number of sectors in a cluster, in a track, and in the FAT. Since this information is used by both DOS and device drivers, the boot record's integrity is essential to the proper functioning of some software. **Do not edit the boot record without a very good reason**.

Information that can be edited is displayed in a single column under the header Boot Record Data. To edit, move the highlighter to the appropriate cell by using the mouse or ↑ and ↓, and enter your change.

## To Edit the Clipboard

1. Pull down the Object menu, and select the **cLipboard** option.
2. Make your changes.

When you copy data, a copy of the marked data is placed in the clipboard. When you paste data, the contents of the clipboard are inserted at the cursor. Thus, editing the contents of the clipboard allows you to copy one thing and paste something else (see "To Copy Marked Data").

The clipboard has a capacity of 4K (4096 bytes). Though you can mark a block larger than this, you cannot copy it.

## To Edit Clusters

1. Pull down the Object menu and select the **Cluster** option, or press **Alt-C**.

2. In the Select Cluster Range dialog box that appears, type the number of the first cluster in the range you want to edit.

3. Type the number of the last cluster in the range you want to edit and select **OK**.

4. Make your changes.

5. Save your changes to disk: Pull down the Edit menu and select the **Write changes** option, or press **Ctrl-W**.

6. Select **Write** in the Write Changes dialog box to confirm saving your changes to disk, or select **Review** to review your changes (this takes you back to step 4).

The Cluster option and Alt-C are not available when the current drive-type setting is Physical. To edit a cluster, the drive type must be set to Logical. Since the drive type can only be set when selecting a drive, reselect the current drive and start the step sequence again. (See "To Select a Drive.")

The Select Cluster Range dialog box displays the current drive and valid cluster numbers for that drive. You can only select clusters on the current drive. To edit clusters located on another drive, you must first select that drive. (See "To Select a Drive.")

To edit clusters, you must be in hex view (clusters can also be viewed, but not edited, in ASCII text view). In hex view, line numbers go down the left side of the screen, hex values (3A, 34, F1, AC, etc.) go across the center of the screen, and ASCII text characters (equivalent to the displayed hex values) go down the right side of the screen. (See Figure 1.) To change to hex view, pull down the View menu and select the **as Hex** option, or press **F2**. (See "To Select a Different View.")

Once in hex view, you can make changes either to the hex values or to their ASCII equivalents. Changes are entered at the cursor. Move the cursor between the hex values area and the ASCII values area

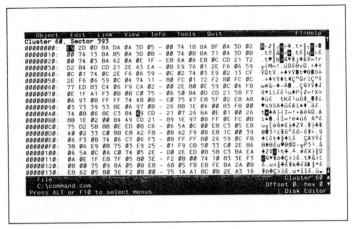

**Figure 1:** Hex view

by clicking either mouse button or by pressing the Tab key. Make sure to enter hex values in the hex values area and ASCII values in the ASCII values area.

## To Edit a Directory

1. Pull down the Object menu and select the **diRectory** option, or press **Alt-R**.

2. In the Change Directory dialog box, select a directory.

3. Make your changes.

4. Save your changes to disk: Pull down the Edit menu and select the W**rite changes** option, or press **Ctrl-W**.

5. Select **Write** in the Write Changes dialog box to confirm saving your changes to disk, or select **Review** to review your changes (this takes you back to step 3).

The Directory option and Alt-R are available only when the current drive-type setting is Logical, not Physical. Since the drive type can only be set when selecting a drive, reselect the current drive and start the step sequence again. (See "To Select a Drive.")

Only the directories on the currently selected drive appear in the Change Directory dialog box. To select a directory located on another drive, you must first select that drive. (See "To Select a Drive.")

A directory can be highlighted for selection in any of the usual ways (scrolling with the mouse or arrow keys) or by using **Speed Search**. To use Speed Search, type the first letter or letters of the directory you want to highlight. Each time you type a letter, the high-light bar jumps to the next directory name beginning with the letter typed. Pressing Ctrl-⌐ cycles the highlight bar through all direc-tories that match the current search string.

Once you have selected a directory, its structure is displayed on the screen, and you can edit any file's name, extension, size, creation date and time, starting cluster, and attributes. Altering a file's start-ing cluster is potentially dangerous, as DOS may no longer be able to find the entire file when needed. A file's attributes can also be changed with the Set Attributes option on the Tools menu.

The directory is laid out in columns and rows. To edit it, move the highlighter to the appropriate cell by using the mouse or the Tab and arrow keys, and enter your change.

## To Edit the FAT (1st Copy)

**Warning**: Since the FAT contains critical information about the file structure of your disk, it is recommended that you do not edit it ex-cept as a last resort.

1. Pull down the Object menu and select the 1st **copy of FAT** option, or press **Alt-F1**.

2. Make your changes.

3. Save your changes to disk: Pull down the Edit menu and select the W**rite changes** option, or press **Ctrl-W**.

4. Toggle on **synchronize FATs** in the Write Changes dialog box to update changes on both copies of the FAT.

5. Select **Write** in the Write Changes dialog box to confirm saving your changes to disk, or select **Review** to review your changes (this takes you back to step 3).

6. Pull down **Rescan** in the Rescan dialog box to display the changes you have just made.

7. Repeat step 1 if necessary.

The FAT (file allocation table) is the means by which DOS keeps track of all the files on a disk. Every cluster on a disk has a corresponding entry in the FAT indicating whether the cluster is in use and, if so, by what file.

As displayed by DISKEDIT, the first position shown in the table is the entry for cluster 2, the next is for cluster 3, and so on from left to right and top to bottom. Clusters 0 and 1 are not represented, as they contain the boot record, partition table, and the FATs, not files. If a cluster's entry shows **0**, the cluster is not in use. If it shows **<BAD>**, the cluster has been marked as bad and will not be used by DOS. If it shows a number other than 0, this is the number of the *next* cluster used by the file. If an entry shows **<EOF>**, this is the *last* cluster used by the file. (See Figure 2.)

To help you navigate, the name of the file containing the high-lighted cluster entry is displayed in the lower-left corner of the screen. If Quick Move is on (see "To Configure DISKEDIT"), all entries belonging to a file are highlighted when the cursor is placed on one of them.

To make changes, type over the current entry:

- Type a number to enter a number.
- Type **E** to enter an <EOF> marker.
- Type **B** to mark a cluster as <BAD>.

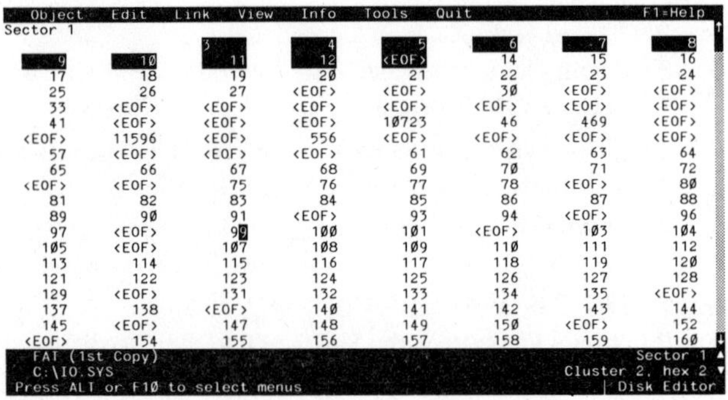

**Figure 2:** A sample selection from a FAT

The highlight is moved by clicking either mouse button on an entry or by using the arrow keys. On some displays, the highlight contains a cursor. Moving left and right to other entries when the cursor is present requires multiple keystrokes.

Because editing the FAT carries with it the risk of scrambling your file structure beyond recognition, **it is recommended that you do not edit the FAT unless absolutely necessary**.

## To Edit the FAT (2nd Copy)

1. Pull down the Object menu and select the 2**nd copy of FAT** option, or press **Alt-F2**.
2. Follow the same steps under "To Edit the FAT (1st Copy)."

DOS creates two copies of the FAT, as there is some security in redundancy. Should the first FAT become corrupted, the second is used. [See "To Edit the FAT (1st Copy)."]

RAM disks have only one FAT. If you are editing a RAM disk, skip step 4.

## To Edit a File

1. Pull down the Object menu and select the **File** option, or press **Alt-F**.
2. Select a file in the Select File dialog box.
3. Make your changes.
4. Save your changes to disk: Pull down the Edit menu and select the W**rite changes** option, or press **Ctrl-W**.
5. Select **Write** in the Write Changes dialog box to confirm saving your changes to disk, or select **Review** to review your changes (this takes you back to step 3).

This function allows you to edit the contents of a file.

To specify a file, type a complete file name and path (if necessary) in the text box at the top of the Select File dialog box or select a file by double-clicking on the Drives, Dirs, and Files lists. Any file on your system can be selected.

To edit a file, you must be in hex view. To change to hex view, pull down the View menu and select the **as Hex** option, or press **F2** (see "To Select a Different View").

Once in hex view, you can make changes either to the hex values or to their ASCII equivalents. Changes are entered at the cursor (as opposed to the highlight). Move the cursor between the hex values area and the ASCII values area by clicking either mouse button or by pressing the Tab key. Make sure to enter hex and ASCII values in the appropriate areas.

## To Edit the Partition Table

**Warning**: As you stand to lose all the data in a partition you edit, it is recommended that you do not edit a partition unless absolutely necessary.

1. Pull down the Object menu and select the **partition Table** option, or press **Alt-A**.
2. Make your changes.
3. Save your changes to disk: Pull down the Edit menu and select the **Write changes** option, or press **Ctrl-W**.
4. Select **Write** in the Write Changes dialog box to confirm saving your changes to disk, or select **Review** to review your changes (this takes you back to step 2).

In the partition table, DOS keeps track of the boundaries of the various partitions on your hard disk. In general, you should make changes to the partition table with the FDISK command in DOS. However, since FDISK does not recognize non-DOS partitions or partitions created by other partitioning software, using DISKEDIT can be a good way to remove such partitions. Keep in mind, however, that when you *resize* a partition, you generally have to reformat it, thereby erasing all data in it.

DISKEDIT displays the partition table in rows and columns. Each row represents one partition. There are six columns.

**System**: the operating system under which the partition was created. Valid entries in this column are listed in Table 1.

**Table 1:** Valid System Entries in the Partition Table

| ENTRY | EXPLANATION |
|---|---|
| DOS-12 | DOS partition with a 12-bit FAT (created by DOS versions prior to 3.0) |
| DOS-16 | DOS partition with a 16-bit FAT (created by DOS versions 3.0 and later) |
| EXTEND | Extended DOS partition. The partition table should have no more than two DOS partitions: the main and the extended. |
| BIGDOS | Primary DOS partition larger than 32Mb (created by Compaq DOS 3.31 and MS-DOS 4.0, 4.01) |
| XENIX | XENIX (IBM UNIX) partition |
| BBT | UNIX–Bad Block Table partition |
| 386-ix | UNIX partition |
| PCIX | PCIX partition |
| HPFS | OS/2 partition |
| Split | Partition created by SplitDrive |
| Speed | Partition created by SpeedStor |
| DM | Partition created by Disk Manager |
| GB | Partition created by GoldenBow VFeature |
| Novell | Novell partition |
| CP/M | CP/M partition |
| ? | Unknown partition |
| Unused | Unused partition |

**Boot**: the active partition (i.e., the partition from which an operating system boots).

**Starting and Ending Locations**: the first and last *physical* sectors of a partition; that is, the starting and ending sectors described in terms of their physical location on the disk—a particular sector on a particular cylinder (track) on a particular side of the disk.

**Relative Sectors**: the "logical" location of the starting sector; that is, the number assigned to the starting sector by the partitioning software.

**Number of Sectors**: the total number of sectors in the partition.

Since both the number of the starting sector and the total number of sectors in a partition may be difficult to calculate, DISKEDIT can do this for you with the Recalculate Partition option on the Tools pull-down menu:

1. In the partitions to be recalculated, set Relative Sectors and Number of Sectors to 0.

2. Highlight the entire row with the mouse or cursor keys.

3. Pull down the Tools menu, and select the **Recalculate Partition** option.

Since the partition table is laid out in rows and columns, editing the table is simply a matter of highlighting the appropriate cell or entry and entering a new value. The highlight can be moved either by clicking with the mouse or by pressing Tab and the arrow keys.

## To Edit Physical Sectors

1. Pull down the Object menu and select the **Physical sector** option, or press **Alt-P**.

2. In the Select Physical Sector Range dialog box that appears, type the number of the cylinder containing the first sector in the range you want to edit.

3. Type the number of the side containing the first sector in the range you want to edit.

4. Type the number of the first sector in the range you want to edit.

5. Enter the total number of sectors in the range you want to view.

6. Make your changes in the View window that appears.

7. Save your changes to disk: Pull down the Edit menu and select the **Write changes** option, or press **Ctrl-W**.

8. Select **Write** in the Write Changes dialog box to confirm saving your changes to disk, or select **Review** to review your changes (this takes you back to step 6).

The essential difference between editing physical and logical sectors is one of identification. Physical sectors are addressed in terms of their physical location on the disk rather than by an integer assigned by DOS for bookkeeping purposes (i.e., a logical location). So, in steps 2, 3, and 4, you identify the first sector in the range you want to edit as a particular sector on a particular track on a particular side of the disk. In step 5, you then specify the size of the range you want to edit.

Since you access sectors by physical, rather than by logical, location, you can use the steps above to view the contents of non-DOS partitions or disks with damaged file or directory structures.

Other than sector identification, editing physical sectors is identical to editing "regular" sectors. (See "To Edit Sectors.")

## To Edit Sectors

1. Pull down the Object menu and select the **Sector** option, or press **Alt-S**.

2. In the Select Sector Range dialog box that appears, type the number of the first sector in the range you want to edit.

3. Enter the number of the last sector in the range you want to edit.

4. Make your changes in the View window that appears.

5. Save your changes to disk: Pull down the Edit menu and select the **Write changes** option, or press **Ctrl-W**.

6. Select **Write** in the Write Changes dialog box to confirm saving your changes to disk, or select **Review** to review your changes (this takes you back to step 4).

The Sector option and Alt-S are available only when the current drive-type setting is Logical, not Physical. Since the drive type can only be set when selecting a drive, reselect the current drive and start the step sequence again. (See "To Select a Drive.")

The Select Sector Range dialog box displays the current drive and the valid sector numbers for that drive. You can only select sectors on the current drive. To edit sectors located on another drive, you must first select that drive. (See "To Select a Drive.")

To edit sectors, you must be in hex view. To change to hex view, pull down the View menu and select the **as Hex** option, or press **F2** (see "To Select a Different View").

Once in hex view, you can make changes either to the hex values or to their ASCII equivalents. Changes are entered at the cursor. Move the cursor between hex values and ASCII values by clicking either mouse button or by pressing Tab. Make sure to enter hex and ASCII values in the appropriate areas.

## To Fill Data

1. Mark the block to be filled (see "To Mark Data").
2. Pull down the Edit menu, and select the Fill command.
3. Enter the fill character.

Data fill allows you to overwrite a marked block from beginning to end with one character.

Some fills cannot be undone. **If the block to be filled spans a sector boundary, you cannot undo the fill**. You receive a warning to this effect when you are prompted for the fill character. Sector boundaries are marked on the screen; just look for the "mile marker": for example, **Cluster 103, Sector 208 or Sector 76**.

The procedure for filling in the FAT differs slightly from filling anywhere else. In step 3, instead of merely choosing the fill character, you have a choice of five ways to fill the block: You can mark the clusters in the block as Unused, as Bad, or as End-of-File marks, or you can overwrite them with a decimal or hex character of your choosing.

## To Link to Corresponding Data

- Pull down the Link menu, and select an appropriate link
  option (file, directory, cluster chain, or partition). These options have function-key equivalents:

  | | |
  |---|---|
  | Link to File | **Ctrl-F** |
  | Link to Directory | **Ctrl-D** |
  | Link to Cluster Chain (FAT) | **Ctrl-T** |

With the link functions, you can move directly from a file to its
entry in the directory or to its entries in the FAT, or vice versa. Although you can make such moves by using the Object menu, linking is faster, as the highlight will always be positioned on the
corresponding file, directory entry, or cluster chain.

The link commands are only available after a file, directory, or FAT
has first been selected for editing from the Object menu. The links
are unavailable (and are grayed out on the Link menu) if a sector,
physical sector, or boot record has been selected for editing.

An object cannot be linked to itself, so while a file is selected, File is
grayed out on the Link menu.

Selecting Partition while the partition table is being edited establishes a link to the boot record corresponding to the highlighted
partition. Unused partitions have no corresponding boot record, so
selecting Partition has no effect.

## To Mark Data (Mark Block)

1. Position the highlight at the beginning of the block to be
   marked.
2. To turn marking on, pull down the Edit menu and select
   the Mark option, or press **Ctrl-B**.
3. Using the arrow keys, move the cursor to the end of the
   block.
4. Repeat step 2 to turn marking off.

Or if you have a mouse,

- Click and hold the left mouse button at the beginning of
  the block, and drag to the end of the block.

When editing with DISKEDIT, data can be manipulated in blocks as well as in discrete units. Data marked as a block can be copied from one place to another, deleted, or overwritten.

## To Select a Drive

**1.** Pull down the Object menu and select the D**rive** option, or press **Alt-D**.

**2.** In the dialog box that appears, specify the drive type in the Type box (Logical or Physical).

**3.** Select a drive from the drive list.

This function selects a drive (either Logical or Physical) whose contents you want to edit or view.

Selecting the Logical drive type makes all drives available by drive letter. The drive list includes all floppy drives, hard-disk partitions (D:, E:, etc.), and drives created with device drivers (RAM disks or encrypted disks created with DISKREET).

Selecting the Physical drive type makes only physical drives (for example, Floppy Disk A:, Floppy Disk B:, and Hard Disk 1) available in the drive list. It does not list logical partitions on a hard disk or drives created with device drivers.

## To Undo Edits

• Pull down the Edit menu and select the U**ndo** command, or press **Ctrl-U**.

This command undoes edits in reverse order—the last edit made is the first one undone.

When using Undo, keep in mind that it has important limitations:

• If you are going to undo a change, you must do it before changes are written to the disk. Once changes are saved, you cannot undo them.

• Changes written across sector boundaries cannot be undone. Sector boundaries are marked on the screen; just look for the "mile marker": **Cluster 103, Sector 208 or Sector 76**, etc.

- The size of the undo buffer is only 512K. Therefore, if you make an edit larger than this, only the last 512K of the edit can be recovered.

## To Use Write To

1. Pull down the Tools menu, and select the W**rite to** option.
2. In the Write dialog box, select how you want to write out the current selection.
3. Select the disk on which to write.
4. Specify the file name, starting cluster, starting sector, or starting physical sector, and select **OK**.

DISKEDIT's Copy command, Paste Over command, and clipboard are adequate for most data-copying situations, but they do have limitations. The clipboard has a 4K capacity, and Copy and Paste Over can only copy data between existing objects. It is occasionally necessary to create *new* objects larger than 4K, such as when you move data from a damaged floppy disk to a new file on your hard disk.

The Write To command creates a new object by writing out a copy of the currently selected object to a destination you specify: a new file or specific clusters, sectors, or physical sectors.

## WINDOW FUNCTIONS

## To Close a Split Window

- Pull down the View menu and select the U**nsplit window** option, or press **Shift-F5**.

Or if you have a mouse,

- Click either mouse button inside the Close Window box on the status bar for the window you want to close (see Figure 3).

Using the mouse allows you to close the window of your choice. The Unsplit Window command, issued either from the menu or with Shift-F5, closes only the *inactive* window. The cursor and highlight appear only in the active window.

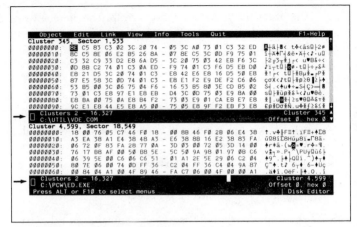

**Figure 3:** Close Window boxes

## To Compare Windows

1.  With split windows on the screen, pull down the Tools menu, and select the **Compare Windows** option.

2.  Repeat as necessary.

The Compare Windows command enables you to compare, byte by byte, the contents of the inactive window with the contents of the active window. It is most useful when the two windows are supposed to hold identical things.

The comparison stops when a mismatch is found. Lengthy comparisons can be terminated by selecting Stop.

## To Link Windows

*   With split windows on the screen, pull down the Link menu, and select the **Window** option.

When windows are linked, highlighting an entry in a FAT in one window displays the corresponding sector in the other window, highlighting a directory entry in one window displays the corresponding file or directory in the other window, and so on.

Links between windows are unidirectional—that is, links are only displayed in the window that was inactive at the time the Window command was issued. Selections must be made in the window that was active when the command was issued. If you switch active windows, links will not be properly updated.

Linked windows are turned off the same way they are turned on: Pull down the Link menu, and select the Windows option. Closing one window does not turn off linked windows. If you resplit the window, the two resulting windows will once again be linked.

## To Resize Split Windows

• Pull down the View menu and select the G**row window** command, or press **Shift-F6**.

or

• Pull down the View menu and select the s**Hrink window** command, or press **Shift-F7**.

Or if you have a mouse,

• Click and hold either mouse button on the status bar dividing the two windows, and drag to a new location.

The most efficient way to resize split windows is to use the mouse. Whether issued through the View menu or by using the function-key combinations, the Grow Window and Shrink Window commands resize the windows only one line at a time.

## To Select a Different View

• Pull down the View menu, and select the appropriate view option:

| Option | Key |
|---|---|
| View **as H**ex | F2 |
| View **as T**ext | F3 |
| View **as D**irectory | F4 |
| View **as FA**T | F5 |

View **as Partition Table**    F6

View **as Boot Record**       F7

If the Auto View option is turned on (See "To Configure DISK-
EDIT"), the program automatically selects the best view. ASCII text
files appear in text view, binary files in hex view, FATs in FAT view,
and so on. If Auto View is turned off, the view is determined by
your data selection. Directories, FATs, partition tables, and boot
records come up in their appropriate views. Data selected as files,
clusters, sectors, or physical sectors always come up in hex view.

You can change from one view to another at any time. However,
some views are incompatible with some selections. The FAT, partition, boot record, and directory views, for example, display gar-
bage when used to view data on the disk outside of these areas.

You can edit in every view except ASCII text view. Though text files
are easier to see in text view, they should be edited in hex view.

## To Split a Window

- Pull down the View menu and select the S**plit window** option, or press **Shift-F5**.

Or if you have a mouse,

- Click either mouse button anywhere on the status bar, and
  drag until the window is sized to your liking.

With two windows open, you can edit two different objects in two
different views, though you can work in only one at a time (the active window). The cursor and the highlight appear only in the
active window.

## To Switch Active/Inactive Windows

- Pull down the View menu and select the s**Witch Window**
  command, or press **Shift-F8**.

Or if you have a mouse,

- Click either mouse button in the window you want to
  make active.

# INFO FUNCTIONS

## To Display Information about the Current Drive

1.  Pull down the Info menu, and select the Drive info option.
2.  Select **OK**, or press **Esc** or ↵ when finished.

The Drive Info option gives information on the currently selected drive. This is the drive selected by the Drive option or the File option on the Object pull-down menu. In addition to the drive name and type, both logical and physical information is displayed. The logical information given is the number of bytes that make up a sector, the number of sectors in a cluster, the number of clusters on the disk, and the type of FAT on the disk. The physical information given is the number of sides and tracks on the disk, the number of sectors in a track, and the number of the drive.

## To Display Information about the Current Object

1.  Pull down the Info menu, and select the Object info option.
2.  Select **OK**, or press **Esc** or ↵ when finished.

The Object Info option provides information about the currently selected object: file, cluster, FAT, directory, etc.

Such information can be useful in many instances. For example, if a cluster containing data goes bad, it is possible to identify the endangered file. If it suddenly is not possible to save a file in the root directory, you can check to see whether the directory already contains its maximum number of files. Or, if you attempt to delete a file and get a message that says "Access denied," you can check to see whether the file is read-only.

## To Map the Current Selection

1.  Pull down the Info menu, and select the Map of object option.
2.  Select **OK**, or press **Esc** or ↵ when finished.

This function maps the amount of used and unused space on the disk and shows the relative size of the current selection (see Figure 4).

The Map of Object option is not available for all possible selections. When the current selection is a FAT, boot record, partition table, or physical sector, the option is unavailable and grayed out on the Info menu. When the current selection is a directory, file, cluster, or sector, the option is available.

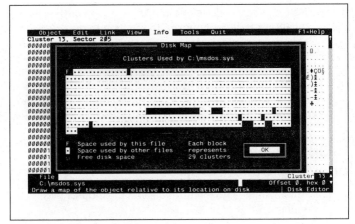

**Figure 4:** Map of a sample file

## TOOLS FUNCTIONS

## To Configure DISKEDIT

1.  Pull down the Tools menu, and select the **cOnfiguration** option.
2.  Toggle selections.
3.  Select **OK** or **Save**.

The DISKEDIT Configuration menu is a dialog box with five possible settings, all toggles.

The **Read Only** setting enables and disables editing. When it is on, editing is off—changes cannot be entered or written to disk—and every option on the Edit pull-down menu, except the Mark option, is grayed out and unavailable.

The **Quick Move** setting affects how quickly DISKEDIT can move from object to selected object. When it is off, 1) the name of the file that contains highlighted data is displayed on the status bar, and 2) in FAT view, when one cluster of a file is highlighted, all other clusters comprising that file are highlighted as well. DISKEDIT requires a little time to constantly track the current file name, so switching is slowed down. Switching is faster when Quick Move is on.

The **Auto View** setting determines how DISKEDIT chooses a view. If it is turned on, the program automatically selects the best view. ASCII text files appear in text view, binary files in hex view, FATs in FAT view, and so on. If Auto View is off, the view is determined by your data selection. Directories, FATs, partition tables, and boot records, when selected from the Object pull-down menu or by using equivalent keystrokes, come up in their appropriate views. Data selected as files, clusters, sectors, or physical sectors always come up in hex view.

The **Quick Links** setting enables linking much like what is available from the Link pull-down menu (see "To Link to Corresponding Data"), though Quick Links is faster. When this setting is on, you can link to corresponding data simply by double-clicking on an entry or by pressing ↵ when an entry is highlighted. Specifically, double-clicking on a cluster in the FAT takes you to the file containing that cluster in directory view. Double-clicking on a file name in directory view takes you to the hex view of that file. Double-clicking in hex view on any byte in use by a file takes you to that file in directory view or to the corresponding cluster in the FAT, depending on a number of different conditions.

The **Character Filters** setting essentially determines how DISK-EDIT displays files in WordStar format. If Show All Characters is selected, such files appear as they do when viewed with the TYPE command in DOS, full of "ASCII noise." If View WordStar Files is selected, such files are readable as if they were regular ASCII text.

Selecting OK puts your settings in effect for the current session only. Selecting Save writes your settings to disk. If you select Save, you are asked to confirm the name of the file that will contain the settings.

## To Consult a Built-in ASCII Table

1. Pull down the Tools menu, and select the A**SCII Table** command.

2. Scroll to see the complete list of characters.

3. Select **OK**, or press **Esc** or ↵ when finished.

DISKEDIT has a built-in ASCII table for reference, showing all 256 ASCII characters and their decimal and hex equivalents. You can scroll the list up and down or jump directly to a character. To jump to a character that appears on the keyboard, simply type the character. To jump to a character not on the keyboard, hold down the Alt key and type the character's decimal equivalent on your keyboard's numeric keypad. (See also "To Do Base Conversion.")

## To Do Base Conversion

1. Pull down the Tools menu, and select the H**ex converter** option.

2. In the Converter dialog box, enter a number, a hex number, or an ASCII character in the appropriate text box.

3. Select **OK**, or press **Esc** or ↵ when finished.

This function converts between hex numbers, decimal numbers (positive integers), and ASCII characters. Entering a value of any type produces equivalents in the other two types. For example, entering the hex value 91 produces its decimal equivalent, 145, and its ASCII character equivalent, £. You are not limited to the 256 ASCII characters and their equivalents, because you can enter decimal numbers ten digits long and hex numbers eight digits long.

The Converter dialog box has three component text boxes: Hex, Decimal, and Character (ASCII). Be sure to enter values in the appropriate box. ASCII characters that appear on the keyboard can be entered simply by typing their keys. To enter an ASCII character that does not appear on the keyboard, hold down the Alt key and type the character's decimal equivalent on your keyboard's numeric keypad.

## To Search for Data

1. Pull down the Tools menu and select the **Find** option, or press **Ctrl-S**.
2. Type the search string in ASCII or hex.
3. Optionally toggle the **Ignore case** switch on or off.
4. Select **Find**.
5. To search for another occurrence of the string, pull down the Tools menu and select the **find aGain** option, or press **Ctrl-G**.

The Find command searches the current selection for the specified string; it is particularly useful for finding misplaced data. The search string can be entered in either ASCII or hex and can be no longer than 48 ASCII characters.

Ignore Case instructs Find to disregard capitalization in its search. Searching for "Linda," for example, will find every consecutive occurrence of the letters l-i-n-d-a without regard to case: "Linda," "LINDA," "LiNdA," and so on. If Ignore Case is turned off, searching for "Linda" will find "Linda" only.

While DISKEDIT is searching, you can interrupt the search by selecting Stop.

After one occurrence of the search has been located, the Find Again option becomes available on the Tools menu.

## To Set File Attributes

1. If you aren't currently editing a directory, pull down the Object menu and select the **DiRectory** option, or press **Alt-R**.
2. Highlight the file or files whose attributes you want to set.
3. Pull down the Tools menu, and select the **set aTtributes** command.
4. In the Change Attributes dialog box, mark each attribute you want to set or clear.
5. Select **OK** when you're finished.
6. To make your changes permanent, pull down the Edit menu and select the **Write changes** option, or press **Ctrl-W**.

This function is essentially identical to the FA (File Attributes) program in the Norton Utilities version 4.5 and can also be found in the FILEFIND program.

To set file attributes, you must be editing a directory in directory view. The file or files whose attributes you want to change must have their entries completely highlighted, from left to right across the screen. If only part of the complete entry is highlighted, the Set Attributes command will be grayed out and unavailable.

Under DOS, there are four file attributes:

**System**: DOS has two system files, named IBMBIO.COM and IBMDOS.COM in PC-DOS and IO.SYS and MSDOS.SYS in MS-DOS. These files make a disk bootable but do not appear in a normal directory listing. If you have formatted a bootable disk and want to recover the space used by the system files (for example, for data storage), remove the system attribute (and the hidden attribute) first. IBMBIO.COM and IBMDOS.COM will then be visible in the directory listing and can be deleted with the DEL command.

**Hidden**: Like the system files, hidden files do not appear in normal directory listings. Turning on the hidden attribute can give you an added measure of security. Similarly, some copy protection schemes write hidden files to your hard disk, which can remain behind after the program has been removed.

**Read-Only**: Files that have the read-only attribute set cannot be altered or deleted.

**Archive**: Used exclusively by backup programs (particularly BACKUP.COM, which comes with DOS) as follows: Only files with the archive attribute set can be backed up. Every time a file is created or modified, its archive attribute is turned on. When a file is backed up, the archive attribute is turned off. Therefore, BACK-UP.COM is able to back up only files that have been added or changed since your last backup.

## To Set File Date and Time

1.  If you aren't currently editing a directory, pull down the Object menu and select the **DiRectory** option, or press **Alt-R**. Then highlight the directory you want to view and select **OK**.

2. Highlight completely (from left to right) the file or files whose date and/or time you want to set.

3. Pull down the Tools menu, and select the **set Date/time** option.

4. In the Set Date/Time dialog box, enter the new date and/or time if you do not want to accept the suggested system date and time.

5. Toggle on the Set Date and/or Set Time boxes.

6. Select **OK**.

7. To make your changes permanent, pull down the Edit menu and select the **Write changes** option, or press **Ctrl-W**.

This function is essentially identical to the FD (File Date) program in the Norton Utilities version 4.5 and can also be found in the FILEFIND program.

To set file dates or times, you must be editing a directory in directory view. The file or files whose dates or times you want to change must have their entries completely highlighted, from left to right across the screen. If only part of the complete entry is highlighted, the Set Date/Time command will be grayed out and unavailable.

After specifying the date and/or time to which the target file(s) are to be set, you still must toggle on the adjacent switches if you want to make the change. This extra step enables you to change the date and not the time, or vice versa.

## QUIT FUNCTIONS

### To Quit DISKEDIT

• Pull down the Quit menu and select the **Quit Disk Editor** option, or press **Ctrl-Q**.

or

• Press **Esc**, and select **Yes** in the Quit Disk Editor dialog box asking for confirmation.

These two methods of exiting DISKEDIT are identical in all but one circumstance. If edits have been made but not written to disk, the Quit Disk Editor option asks whether you want to save the edits and then exits the program. If the edits alter a directory, FAT, partition table, or boot record, it also asks whether you want to rescan the disk to display current information. Pressing Esc to exit produces the same prompts but does not exit the program.

## To Use Shell to DOS

- Pull down the Quit menu, and select the **Shell to DOS** option.

This function allows you to exit temporarily to the DOS prompt. Type **EXIT** and press ↵ to return to DISKEDIT.

## • SYNTAX

**DISKEDIT (***drive:***) (***filespec***) (/***options***)**

***drive***: is the drive to be edited. If *drive:* is not specified, the current drive is used.

***filespec*** starts DISKEDIT with *filespec* selected as the current object.

The options are the following:

**/M** starts DISKEDIT in Maintenance Mode. Looks at data by file or physical sector (without regard to the operating system's data organization).

**/X:(***drive***)** excludes the drive you specify from use. For Zenith DOS users only.

**See Also**    FILEFIND

# DISKMON

DISKMON enables you to park the heads on your hard disk, display a disk activity light, and write-protect your disks so that you are prompted for confirmation each time a program attempts to write to a protected file or area of a disk.

● **UPGRADE INFORMATION**   DISKMON is new to version 5.0 and has no predecessor in version 4.5.

## To Park Your Hard Disk

   1. Start DISKMON.
   2. Select **Disk Park** in the Disk Monitor dialog box.
   3. Shut off your machine.

Disk Park positions the read/write heads over an unused area of the disk and gently lowers them to the disk surface. This helps guard against damage and data loss. If you do not have a hard disk whose heads park automatically when the power is shut off, be sure to use Disk Park before you move your machine.

## To Turn the Disk Light On or Off

   1. Start DISKMON.
   2. Select **Disk Light** in the Disk Monitor dialog box.
   3. Select **On** or **Off**.

Disk Light enables (or disables) a drive activity indicator that monitors the activity of all drives on your system. When a drive on your system is accessed, the drive letter flashes in the upper-right corner of your screen. This is particularly useful for monitoring RAM disks, network drives, and for users who place their machines on the floor. Note, however, that Disk Light does not work in graphics mode.

## To Use Disk Protect

1. Start DISKMON.
2. Select **Disk Protect** in the Disk Monitor dialog box.
3. In the Disk Protect dialog box, select an area to protect.
4. In the Files list, specify the files you want to protect.
5. In the Exceptions list, specify any exempted files.
6. Toggle **Allow Floppy Access** on.
7. Select **On** or **Off**.

Disk Protect write-protects files and selected areas of all drives on your system. Whenever a program (DOS or any application) attempts to write to a protected file or area, the user is asked to allow or disallow the action. This is particularly useful as protection against accidental deletion of important files and as protection against many viruses (for example, those that attempt to modify your COMMAND.COM file or write hidden files to your hard disk).

In step 3, selecting System Areas protects all partition tables, boot records, and DOS system files (IBMBIO.COM and IBMDOS.COM or IO.SYS and MSDOS.SYS).

In step 4, selecting Files protects the specified groups of files. Files are specified by extension only (*.*, *.COM, *.BAT, etc.).

In step 5, the Excepted Files list specifies files that are not protected. You may specify up to 20 file names as exceptions. Wildcards are allowed.

Selecting Entire Disk protects empty disk space on every drive, all partition tables, boot records, DOS system files, FATs, and directories, as well as the specified files.

Toggling Allow Floppy Access on allows you to format a floppy without DISKMON asking for confirmation. If this option is toggled off and you attempt to format a disk, you will be prompted for confirmation often, which may annoy you.

If you choose to protect only the system areas, skip steps 4 and 5.

## To Quit DISKMON

- Select **Quit** in the Disk Monitor dialog box, or press **Esc**.

## • SYNTAX

**DISKMON (/*options*)**

The options are the following:

**/STATUS** displays the current state of the Disk Light and Disk Protect functions.

**/PROTECT+** turns on Disk Protect. Since DISKMON always remembers your selections for protected areas, file lists, etc., the last active settings are used.

**/PROTECT-** turns off Disk Protect.

**/LIGHT+** turns on Disk Light.

**/LIGHT-** turns off Disk Light.

**/PARK** parks the read/write heads on all hard drives.

**/UNINSTALL** removes DISKMON from memory.

• **NOTES** DISKMON is a Terminate and Stay Resident (TSR) program that occupies approximately 8K of memory. It can be removed from memory by using the /UNINSTALL option at the command line or by turning off both Disk Light and Disk Protect. Keep in mind, though, that you will not be able to remove DISK-MON if you load another TSR while DISKMON is resident.

# DISKREET
## The File Encryption Program

DISKREET offers two forms of file encryption to protect confidential data; it can encrypt files individually or create encrypted drives called NDisks. A password is required to access all encrypted data.

To use DISKREET, the DISKREET.SYS driver must be placed in your CONFIG.SYS file:

**device=** *path* **\ DISKREET.SYS**

See the Appendix if you need help with loading device drivers.

● **UPGRADE INFORMATION**    DISKREET is new to version 5.0 and has no predecessor in version 4.5.

## To Adjust the Size of an NDisk

1.  Start DISKREET.
2.  In the Diskreet dialog box, select **Disks**.
3.  In the Diskreet Disks dialog box, highlight the NDisk you want to resize.
4.  Pull down the Disk menu, and select the A**djust size** option.
5.  Enter the NDisk's password.
6.  In the Adjust NDisk Size dialog box, select **Expand** or **Shrink** to size the NDisk accordingly.
7.  Select **Proceed** after you read the warning.
8.  Select the amount of disk space to add to or subtract from the NDisk.

This function adjusts the amount of space an NDisk occupies on its host drive.

In step 8, you have four options:

•  Select the **Maximum** adjustment to increase the size of the NDisk so that it occupies all remaining disk space on its host drive or to decrease it so that it is as small as possible (approximately 2K).

- Select the **Half** adjustment to add to the NDisk half of the remaining disk space on the host drive or to cut the NDisk approximately in half.

- Select the **Quick** adjustment to increase or decrease the NDisk by an amount suggested by DISKREET.

- Select the **Specific Size** adjustment to increase or decrease the NDisk by a specific number of kilobytes.

## To Change the Main Password

1. Start DISKREET.

2. In the Diskreet dialog box, select **Disks**.

3. Pull down the Options menu, and select the C**hange main password** option.

4. Select **OK** to acknowledge the Change Main Password dialog box.

5. Enter a new main password.

6. Reenter this password to validate your entry in the previous step.

The main password is used to set DISKREET program options and is different from the ones used to encrypt individual files. Specifically, the main password is needed to set start-up options and auto-close timeouts, and to lock the keyboard and display.

When you first use DISKREET, there is no main password. If prompted for it, simply press ↵. The main password remains "null" until you change it. This new password remains, even in different DISKREET sessions, until you change it again.

Unlike passwords assigned to encrypted files, all is not lost if you forget the main password. To reset the password to "null," delete the DISKREET.INI file found in the Norton Utilities directory and reboot the machine. This also resets all DISKREET options to their original defaults.

## To Change an NDisk's Password or Description

1. Start DISKREET.
2. In the Diskreet dialog box, select **Disks**.
3. In the Diskreet Disks dialog box, highlight the NDisk whose password or description you want to change.
4. Pull down the Disk menu, and select the **change disk Password** option.
5. In the Change NDisk Password dialog box, select **Proceed**.
6. Enter the NDisk's current password.
7. In the Change NDisk Password dialog box, select **Change** to change the NDisk's *description*.
8. In the Change NDisk Description dialog box, enter a new description or press ⏎ to leave the description unchanged.
9. Enter a new password for the NDisk.
10. Reenter the password for verification.
11. In the Change NDisk Password dialog box, select **Full** to change the password and rewrite the NDisk, or select **Quick** to change the password only.

In step 11, the Full option assigns the new password to the NDisk and, for maximum security, reencrypts it. The Quick option, by contrast, only assigns the new password. It is unlikely that you run any risk by using the Quick option, though if security is a major concern, use Full instead. Keep in mind that reencrypting a large NDisk can be time consuming.

## To Change System Settings

1. Start DISKREET.
2. In the Diskreet dialog box, select **Disks**.
3. Pull down the Options menu, and select the **System settings** option.
4. If prompted, enter the main password.

5. In the System Settings dialog box, optionally toggle the **Do not load the NDisk Manager** option on.

6. Select the number of drive letters to assign to NDisks.

7. Select **OK**.

8. Select **Reset** to reboot the computer and to put the new options into effect.

In step 5, the **Do not load the NDisk Manager** option is off by default and should remain that way unless memory is tight. Toggling this option on saves approximately 50K by deactivating the DISKREET.SYS driver loaded in your CONFIG.SYS file. However, it prevents you from using any of DISKREET's NDisk functions.

In step 6, you are effectively selecting the number of NDisks that can be opened simultaneously, since each open NDisk must be assigned a drive letter. (See "To Create an NDisk" and "To Open an NDisk.")

## To Close All Open NDisks

• Pull down the Disk menu and select the **Close all** option, or press **Alt-C**.

or

1. Pull down the Options menu, and select the **Keyboard & screen lock** option.

2. If prompted, enter the Main password.

3. In the Keyboard and Screen Lock Settings dialog box, toggle the **Enable Quick-Close** option on.

4. In the Quick Close/Lock Hot Key box, select a hotkey combination and then select **OK**.

5. Press the hotkey combination selected in step 4.

All NDisks are automatically closed if the machine loses power or is rebooted.

## To Close a Particular NDisk

•   In the Diskreet Disks dialog box, highlight the NDisk you want to close and select **Close**.

## To Create an NDisk

1.  Start DISKREET.
2.  In the Diskreet dialog box, select **Disks**.
3.  In the Diskreet Disks dialog box, select the M**ake** option.
4.  Select the drive on which data in the NDisk is to be stored, and select **OK**.
5.  In the Make NDisk on Drive dialog box and at the File Name prompt, enter the name of the NDisk.
6.  At the Description prompt, enter a description of the NDisk.
7.  In the Audit box, choose when you want to see audit information.
8.  In the Encryption box, choose a method of encryption.
9.  In the Password Prompting box, choose how you want to be prompted for the NDisk's password when the NDisk is opened.
10. Select **OK**.
11. In the Select NDisk Size dialog box, specify the size of the NDisk.
12. In the Enter New Password dialog box, enter a password six or more characters long.
13. Reenter the password for verification.
14. Select **OK** after you read the caution.
15. In the Make an NDisk dialog box, select a drive letter for the NDisk.

To use any of DISKREET's NDisk functions, the driver DISKREET-.SYS must be loaded in your CONFIG.SYS file. (If you need help doing this, see the Appendix.)

An NDisk is an encrypted logical disk drive. As it is assigned a drive letter, an NDisk can be addressed like any other logical or physical drive installed on your system. The difference is that all data copied to an NDisk are encrypted, and the NDisk itself is secured with a password. To be accessed, an NDisk must be "opened" (see the section "To Open an NDisk"). When "closed," data in an NDisk cannot be accessed and is secure. **Do not forget the password that you have assigned an NDisk**! Without the password, all data in the NDisk is inaccessible.

NDisks use space on other drives installed on your system to store data. In step 4, you specify the drive on which NDisk data is stored.

An NDisk is treated as a file by DOS. The name you enter for the NDisks in step 5, therefore, must conform to DOS file-name conventions (a maximum of eight characters, with no spaces). The file is hidden, and DISKREET automatically appends the extension .@#! to the file name.

In step 7, there is one option in the Audit box: **Show audit info when opened**. When it is toggled on and you open an NDisk, DISKREET displays the number of times the NDisk has been opened, when the NDisk was last opened, when the NDisk password was last changed, and the number of failed attempts to open the NDisk.

In step 8, there are two methods of encryption you can choose from. The Fast proprietary method is adequate for any normal use. The DES encryption method is more secure and is slower than the proprietary method.

In step 9, there are four options you can choose from:

- Select **Beep only** if you want only to be beeped for a password when an NDisk is opened.

- Select **Pop-up prompt only** if you always want to enter an NDisk's password in a dialog box. Dialog boxes, however, may conflict with graphical interfaces or screens.

- Select **Choose automatically** to have DISKREET choose whether to prompt you for a password with a dialog box or with just a beep. This prevents conflicts with graphical screens.

- Select **Manually open only** if you want to disable automatic opening of NDisks ( in AUTOEXEC.BAT files or

when NDisks are accessed for the first time, for example).
(See "To Open an NDisk" and "To Set Start-up Options.")

In step 10, there are three options: An NDisk can occupy all the
available space on the disk on which it resides, it can occupy half
the available space, or you can specify an NDisk's size in kilobytes.

In step 15, select a drive letter for the NDisk. By default, only one
drive letter is available (the next in the sequence on your system).
This means that, although you can create more than one NDisk,
only one can be open at a time. To have multiple NDisks open
simultaneously, more drive letters have to be made available, and
different drive letters must be assigned to different NDisks. To
make more drive letters available, see "To Change System Settings."

Once an NDisk is created, it is automatically opened and appears in
the list in the Diskreet Disks dialog box.

## To Decrypt a File

1. Start DISKREET.
2. In the Diskreet dialog box, select **Files** or **Disks**.
3. Pull down the File menu, and select the D**ecrypt** option.
4. In the Select File to Decrypt dialog box, select a file you
   want to decrypt.
5. Enter the password for this file.
6. Select **OK** to confirm completion.

If you select **Files** in step 2, you do not have to select the File pull-
down menu in step 3, as it is selected for you. In any DISKREET
session, steps 1 and 2 are unnecessary after you have encrypted or
decrypted one file or performed one NDisk operation.

In step 4, select a file by entering a file name at the **File Name:**
prompt or by selecting from the Drives, Dirs, and Files lists.

## To Delete an NDisk

1. Start DISKREET.
2. In the Diskreet dialog box, select **Disks**.

3. In the Diskreet Disks dialog box, highlight the NDisk you want to delete.

4. Pull down the Disk menu, and select the **Delete** option.

5. If you are certain you want to delete the NDisk, select **Delete** in the Warning dialog box.

## To Edit an NDisk

1. Start DISKREET.

2. In the Diskreet dialog box, select **Disks**.

3. In the Diskreet Disks dialog box, highlight the NDisk you want to edit and select **Edit**.

4. Enter the password for this NDisk.

5. Follow the steps in the section "To Create an NDisk" to change the NDisk's file name, description, method of encryption, audit information, and password prompting.

6. In the Options box, optionally toggle the **Write protection** option on.

7. Select **OK** after you have made your changes.

Editing an NDisk, as explained in step 5, allows you to change the configuration you entered when you created the NDisk.

In addition, in step 6, you can write-protect your NDisk, thereby protecting its data from accidental deletion or alteration.

## To Encrypt a File

1. Start DISKREET.

2. In the Diskreet dialog box, select **Files** or **Disks**.

3. Pull down the File menu and select the **Encrypt** option, or press **Alt-E**.

4. In the Select Files to Encrypt dialog box, select the file(s) to be encrypted and then select **OK**.

5. In the File Encryption dialog box, type the name of the new, encrypted file and select **OK**, or just select **OK** to accept the suggested file name.

6. Enter a password of six or more characters.

7. Reenter this password to confirm it.

8. Select **OK** to confirm completion of the encryption.

**Do not forget the password you assign to an encrypted file!** If you do, the file's data cannot be accessed.

If you select Files in step 2, you do not have to select the File pull-down menu in step 3, as it is selected for you. In any DISKREET session, steps 1 and 2 are unnecessary after you have encrypted or decrypted one file or performed one NDisk operation.

In step 4, select file(s) by entering a file name (wildcards are OK) at the **File Name:** prompt or by selecting from the Drives, Dirs, and Files lists. Although you can select more than one file at a time (for example, *.DOC), the files are not encrypted into separate files but all together into one file.

## To Lock the Keyboard and Blank the Display

1. Pull down the Options menu, and select the **Keyboard & screen lock** option.

2. Enter the main password if prompted to do so.

3. In the Keyboard & Screen Lock Settings dialog box, toggle the **Enable Locking** option on.

4. In the Quick Close/Lock Hot Key box, select a hotkey combination.

5. Select **OK**.

6. To blank the screen and lock the keyboard, hit the hotkey combination.

7. To unblank and unlock, enter the main password.

Steps 1 through 5 are only necessary once. After you go through them once, the keyboard can be locked and the screen blanked at any time and in any application by hitting the hotkey combination.

## To Open an NDisk

1. Start DISKREET.

2. In the Diskreet dialog box, select **Disks**.

3.   In the Diskreet Disks dialog box, highlight the NDisk you want to open and select **Open**.

4.   In the Open an NDisk dialog box, select a drive letter for the NDisk.

5.   Enter the password for the NDisk.

Skip steps 1 and 2 if you are already in a DISKREET session and the Diskreet Disks dialog box is already on the screen.

To access data within an NDisk or to add data to an NDisk, the NDisk must be open. Data in an open NDisk is still encrypted, though accessible.

An NDisk can be opened automatically when the machine is booted or the first time its drive letter is called. In both cases, you still have to enter the NDisk's password. (See "To Set Start-up Options.")

Open NDisks appear with check marks beside them on the Diskreet Disks list of NDisks.

## To Quit DISKREET

•   Select the Quit! menu, or press **Esc**.

## To Search Floppy Disks for NDisks

1.   Pull down the Disk menu and select the S**earch floppies** option, or press **Alt-S**.

2.   In the Search Floppies dialog box, select the floppy drive you want to search for.

When DISKREET first starts, only NDisks that are on a hard disk are displayed in the Diskreet Disks dialog box. To work with NDisks that are on floppies (i.e., to complete the list), follow the procedure above.

## To Set Auto-close Timeouts

1.   Pull down the Options menu, and select the A**uto-close timeouts** option.

2.   Enter the main password.

**3.** In the Set Auto Close Timeouts dialog box, toggle the **Enable** option on, and specify the duration of the auto-close timeout.

**4.** Select **OK**.

This function automatically closes all NDisks if no keyboard activity is detected in the specified amount of time. This is not a usual closure, however. When you reopen an NDisk, all other NDisks closed by the timeout are also reopened. (See "To Close an NDisk" and "To Open an NDisk.")

In step 3, the duration of the timeout may be set anywhere from 0 to 59 minutes.

## To Set File Encryption Options

**1.** Start DISKREET.

**2.** In the Diskreet dialog box, select **Files** or **Disks**.

**3.** Pull down the File menu, and select the **File options** option.

**4.** In the File Encryption Options dialog box and in the Encryption Method box, select a method of encryption.

**5.** Optionally toggle on any of the four encryption options.

**6.** Select **OK** to set these options for the current session only, or select **Save** to set options for both current and future sessions.

If you select **Files** in step 2, you do not have to select the File pull-down menu in step 3, as it is selected for you. Steps 1 and 2 are unnecessary if setting file encryption options is not the first thing you do in a DISKREET session.

In step 4, there are two methods of encryption you can choose from. The Fast proprietary method is quite fast and is adequate for any normal use. The DES encryption method is more secure and is slower than the proprietary method.

In step 5, there are four options you can choose from; the meaning of the first three is fairly self-evident: **Wipe/Delete original files after encryption**, **Set Encrypted file to Hidden**, and **Set Encrypted file to Read-Only**. Select the fourth option, **Use the**

**same password for the entire session**, if you are going to encrypt more than one file and want to use the same password for each. (See "To Encrypt a File"; you will skip steps 6 and 7 for every file you encrypt after the first.)

## To Set Security Options

1. Pull down the Options menu, and select the **Security** option.
2. In the Security Options dialog box, select how you want to dispose of discarded NDisk data.

In step 2, you must choose what to do with NDisk data after an NDisk is deleted. There are three options:

- Select **Quick Clear** to leave encrypted data on the disk where it will eventually be overwritten.
- Select **Overwrite** to have data overwritten once.
- Select **Security Wipe** to have data overwritten according to Department of Defense specifications.

## To Set Start-up (Automatic Open) Options

1. Pull down the Options menu, and select the **startup Disks** option.
2. In the Startup NDisks box, highlight the drive letter representing the NDisk you want to be opened automatically and select **Edit**.
3. In the All NDisks dialog box, highlight the NDisk you want to be opened automatically (and assigned to the letter chosen in step 2), and select **OK**.
4. In the Startup NDisks dialog box, choose whether you want to have the NDisk opened when the machine is booted or when the NDisk is first accessed.
5. Select **OK**.
6. In the Startup NDisks dialog box, select **OK**.

NDisks can always be opened manually (see "To Open an NDisk"). They can be opened automatically when the computer is (re)booted or when the drive letter of a closed NDisk is addressed.

## • SYNTAX

### DISKREET (/*options*)

The options are the following:

**/ENCRYPT:*filespec*** encrypts the file or files specified by *filespec*.

**/DECRYPT:*file*** decrypts the specified file.

**/PASSWORD:*password*** supplies the necessary password. Use this option in combination with /ENCRYPT and /DECRYPT.

**/SHOW :*drive*** unhides all NDisks on the specified drive.

**/HIDE :*drive*** hides all NDisks on the specified drive.

**/CLOSE** closes all open NDisks.

**/OFF** deactivates the DISKREET.SYS device driver.

**/ON** reactivates the DISKREET.SYS device driver.

## • NOTES
If you are running Windows 3.0, a number of DISK-REET's functions will not work—specifically, Auto-open, Quick-close, and Auto-close Timeouts—which means you must actually run DISKREET to open or close NDisks.

If you are using a RAM disk, such as VDISK, the DISKREET.SYS driver should be placed *after* the RAM disk driver in your CONFIG.SYS file. Placing DISKREET.SYS before a RAM disk driver will probably cause a conflict in which the RAM disk and NDisk try to use the same drive. (If you need help with loading device drivers in CONFIG.SYS, see the Appendix.)

# DISKTOOL

DISKTOOL is a collection of six functions that can fix problems ranging from the fairly common to the catastrophic. Specifically, you can make a nonbootable disk bootable, restore the damage done by the DOS RECOVER program, reformat an error-laden disk without loss of data, mark specific clusters as bad (or good), and save critical system information on a separate disk.

● **UPGRADE INFORMATION**   Three of the six DISKTOOL functions—Make a Disk Bootable, Revive a Defective Diskette, and Recover from DOS's Recover—come directly from the Norton Disk Doctor in version 4.5. The other three functions—Mark a Cluster, Create Rescue Disk, and Restore Rescue Disk—are new to version 5.0.

## To Create a Rescue Disk

1.  Start DISKTOOL.
2.  Select **Continue** after reading the introductory screen.
3.  Highlight **Create Rescue Disk** on the Procedures list.
4.  Select **Proceed**.
5.  Select **OK** after you read the information screen.
6.  Select the disk on which you will store rescue information.
7.  Insert a disk in the indicated drive.
8.  When the operation is complete, select **OK** to return to the Disk Tools main screen.

Create Rescue Disk stores vital disk information on a separate floppy. Specifically, it stores a copy of the boot record, partition table, and CMOS information. Your system's internal hardware configuration, number and kind of drives installed, kind of graphics installed, amount of memory, etc., are stored in a CMOS (Complementary Metal Oxide Semiconductor, a special kind of chip). This information is retained even when your computer's power is off, as it is backed up by a battery. Only 286, 386, and 486 machines store setup information in CMOS; XTs do not. If you lose any of this information, it can be restored to your machine from the rescue disk. (See "To Restore the Rescue Disk.")

## To Make a Disk Bootable

1. Start DISKTOOL.

2. Select **Continue** after reading the introductory screen.

3. Highlight **Make a Disk Bootable** on the Procedures list.

4. Select **Proceed**.

5. Select the drive you want to make bootable. (If you select a floppy drive, insert the disk to be made bootable in the drive indicated and select **OK**.)

6. Insert a DOS disk in the drive indicated and select **OK**— this may not be necessary on some configurations. (If you have a floppy drive, reinsert the disk to be made bootable in the drive indicated and select **OK**.)

7. Select **OK** when the operation is complete to return to the Disk Tools main screen.

If you have ever tried to make a bootable floppy disk by using the SYS command in DOS, you have probably encountered the following problem: DOS reports that there is not enough room for the system even though the disk contains only a few small files. The problem is that the DOS system files must sit in a particular place at the beginning of the disk—cluster 2 and the following clusters. The first file copied to a disk not formatted by the system, however, sits in cluster 2, so SYS reports insufficient room *because there is really a file in the way*. The Make a Disk Bootable function relocates data files at the beginning of the disk and copies the system files to the area beginning at cluster 2.

Make a Disk Bootable also works with hard disks, though it is less likely that you will need to use it with them. Since the function always reads the DOS system files from a floppy, it is possible to replace the system files already on your hard disk with system files from a different version of DOS.

## To Mark a Cluster (as Good or Bad)

1. Start DISKTOOL.
2. Select **Continue** after reading the introductory screen.
3. Highlight **Mark a Cluster** on the Procedures list.
4. Select **Proceed**.
5. Select **OK** after you read the information screen.
6. Select the drive on which to mark clusters. (If you've selected a floppy drive, insert the target disk in the indicated drive and select **OK**.)
7. In the Mark Cluster dialog box, enter the number of the cluster you want to mark at the **Mark Cluster:** prompt.
8. Select **Good** or **Bad** in the **Mark as:** box.
9. Select **OK**.
10. When the operation is complete, select **OK** to return to the Disk Tools main screen.

If you are able to identify a cluster that has gone bad, you can remove it from use by DOS with the Mark a Cluster function. If, however, the cluster in question contains data, use the Norton Disk Doctor II's Surface Test instead. This moves the data from the damaged cluster to a healthy one. (See also the NDD section.)

Mark a Cluster can also mark bad clusters as good, thereby returning them to use. Since casually reinstating a cluster marked as bad by DOS or some other disk utility may be hazardous to your data, use this function with care.

## To Quit DISKTOOL

- Select **Quit** in the Disk Tools dialog box, or press **Esc**.

## To Recover from DOS's Recover

1. Start DISKTOOL.
2. Select **Continue** after reading the introductory screen.
3. Highlight **Recover from DOS's Recover** on the Procedures list.

4. Select **Proceed**.

5. Select **OK** when you are finished reading the information screen.

6. Select the drive you want to "fix." (Insert the "damaged" floppy in the indicated drive and select **OK**.)

7. Select **OK** after you read the warning screen.

8. Select **Yes** if you are absolutely sure you want to continue.

9. When the operation is complete, select **OK** to return to the Disk Tools main screen.

The RECOVER program in DOS is intended to recover data on disks whose directory structure has been corrupted. It ends up doing more harm than good, though, because it eliminates all subdirectories and renames all files, numbering them sequentially beginning with 0.

Recover from DOS's Recover has two uses:

• Use it *after* you have run DOS's RECOVER to return your disk to its pre-RECOVER condition (or at least a good approximation thereof).

• Use it *instead* of DOS's RECOVER to repair a disk with a damaged directory structure.

## To Restore the Rescue Disk

1. Start DISKTOOL.

2. Select **Continue** after reading the introductory screen.

3. Highlight **Restore Rescue Disk** on the Procedures list.

4. Select **Proceed**.

5. Select **Yes** when you are absolutely sure you want to proceed.

6. Select the kind of information you want to restore (boot record, partition table, CMOS), and select **OK**.

7. Select the drive from which to restore information.

8. Insert the rescue disk in the indicated drive.

9. When the operation is complete, select **OK** to return to the Disk Tools main screen.

If you lose all or part of your boot record or partition table because of disk failure or careless meddling with the DISKEDIT program, you can restore this critical information and perhaps prevent the loss of most or all of your data.

If your CMOS information is lost (probably due to the death of the battery supplying power to the CMOS), you can restore this information instead of running your Setup program.

## To Revive a Defective Disk

1. Start DISKTOOL.
2. Select **Continue** after reading the introductory screen.
3. Highlight **Revive a Defective Diskette** on the Procedures list.
4. Select **Proceed**.
5. Select the drive you want to revive.
6. Insert the damaged disk in the indicated drive and select **OK**.
7. When the operation is complete, select **OK** to return to the Disk Tools main screen.

The Revive a Defective Diskette function can repair the bad clusters or sectors that may appear on your disks after they have been in use for a while. It reformats your disks *but without destroying any data*. Use this function if you get data-read errors on a floppy that had been in good working order. You may also want to use the Norton Disk Doctor II's Surface Test. (See also the NDD section.)

# FILEFIND

FILEFIND is a multifaceted program. Its primary purpose is to find lost or misplaced files. It is also able to find directories and ASCII text; view files; change file attributes, dates, and times; and perform other related, miscellaneous tasks.

● **UPGRADE INFORMATION**   FILEFIND is an improved version of the FF (File Find) program in version 4.5. It also has the functions, to a greater or lesser extent, of four other programs in version 4.5: FA (File Attributes), TS (Text Search), FD (File Date and Time), and FS (File Size).

## To Change File Attributes

1.  Pull down the Commands menu, and select the **set At-tributes** option. The Change Attributes dialog box appears.
2.  In the Set Attributes box, select whether you want to change attributes of the highlighted file or of every file on the list.
3.  Select the attributes you want to set or clear.
4.  Select **OK**.
5.  Select **OK** again to confirm the changes made.

The FA (File Attributes) command in version 4.5 is contained within FILEFIND. Although it is also possible to change file attributes by using the DISKEDIT program (see "To Change File Attributes" in DISKEDIT), using FILEFIND is preferable, as it is more precise— you are more likely to make a serious error while editing a directory.

This option is only available when a file list appears in the FileFind dialog box (i.e., after you have run a find or search).

## To Change File Dates and Times

1.  Pull down the Commands menu, and select the **set Date/Time** option. The Set Date/Time dialog box appears.

2. In the Set Attributes box, select whether you want to change only the highlighted file or every file on the file list.

3. To change the time, toggle the **Set the time to:** option on, and enter a new time.

4. To change the date, toggle the **Set the date to:** option on, and enter a new date.

5. Select **OK**.

6. Select **OK** again to confirm the changes made.

The FD (File Date and Time) command in version 4.5 is contained within FILEFIND. Although it is also possible to change file dates and times by using the DISKEDIT program (see "To Change File Dates and Times" in DISKEDIT), using FILEFIND is preferable, as it is more precise—you are more likely to make a serious error while editing a directory.

This option is only available when a file list appears in the FileFind dialog box (i.e., after you have run a find or search).

## To Configure the File List

1. Pull down the List menu and select the S**et list display** option, or press **Ctrl-F**. The List Display dialog box appears.

2. In the List Format box, select how much file information you want to display.

3. In the Sort Criterion box, choose how you want to sort found files.

4. In the Sort Order box, choose whether you want sorted files to be listed in ascending or descending order.

5. Select **OK**.

You can sort the file list either before or after a search has been run.

In step 2, there are five options: You can display only the names of found files; file names and attributes; file names and sizes; file names, dates, and times; or file names, sizes, dates, and attributes (the default).

In step 3, found files can be sorted by file name, extension, date and time, size, or can be left unsorted. If you choose the Unsorted option, omit step 4. The Ascending and Descending options will have no effect.

## To Create a Batch File

1. Pull down the List menu and select the **Create batch** option, or press **Ctrl-B**.

2. In the Create Batch File dialog box and at the **Save the list to:** prompt, enter the name of the batch file you want to create.

3. Optionally toggle the **Save full path** and **Directory title line** options on.

4. At the **Text to put before file names:** prompt, optionally enter the text you want to put before file names in the batch file.

5. At the **Text to put after file names:** prompt, optionally enter the text you want to put after file names in the batch file.

6. At the **Text to put before directory lines:** prompt, optionally enter the text you want to put before directory names in the batch file.

7. Select **OK**.

The Create Batch command is unavailable until there is a file list in the FileFind dialog box (i.e., until you run a find or search).

This command allows you to create a batch file from the file list that results from a find or search. It is particularly useful for copying, deleting, or even running a particular group of files. Be certain, therefore, to define carefully the scope and condition of your search, as every file on the file list will be included in the batch file created.

In step 3, the Save Full Path option causes every file in the batch file to have its complete path attached (C:\NU50\FILEFIND.EXE, as opposed to FILEFIND.EXE). Files are grouped by directory both in the file list and in resulting batch files. The Directory Title Line option causes the directory name for each of these groupings to be included in the created batch file.

Text entered in step 4 appears before each file name in the created batch file. Enter DOS commands here. For example, entering **del** produces

> **del filename.ext**

for each file name that appears in the batch file.

Text entered in step 5 appears after each file name in the batch file. Enter DOS command arguments or parameters here. For example, if you entered **copy** in step 4, enter the target directory here:

> **C:\newdir**

This produces

> **copy filename.ext c:\newdir**

for each file name that appears in the batch file.

Text entered in step 6 appears before directory names in the batch file. Enter DOS directory commands here. For example, entering **cd\** produces

> **cd\ c:\directry**

for every directory listed in the batch file. If the Directory Title Line option in step 3 is toggled off, omit step 6.

## To Find a File or Files

1. In the FileFind dialog box, enter a file name and path (the path is optional; wildcards are OK) at the **File Name:** prompt.

2. Specify the search scope (the default drive only, the default directory, or on more than one drive), and optionally specify the search conditions (narrow the scope). See below for explanations.

3. Select **Start** to start the search, and select **OK** when it is finished.

**To Search the Default Drive Only:**

1. In the FileFind dialog box, select the **Entire Disk** option.
2. Pull down the File menu and select the D**rive** option, or press **Ctrl-D**.
3. In the Change Drive dialog box, select the new default drive.
4. Pull down the Search menu and select the **Search drives** option, or press **Alt-D**.
5. In the Drives to Search dialog box, select the **Default drive** option.

Default Drive is the default setting in the Drives to Search box in every new FILEFIND session. Therefore, omit steps 4 and 5 if you have not changed this setting in the current session.

**To Search the Default Directory (and Its Subordinates):**

1. In the FileFind dialog box, select the **Current directory only** option, or select the **Current directory and below** option to search the default directory and those directories below it.
2. Pull down the File menu and select the di**Rectory** option, or press **Ctrl-R**.
3. In the Change Directory dialog box, enter the new directory and path at the **Current Directory** prompt or select it from the Drives and Sub-Directories lists.

If the default directory is already properly set, omit steps 2 and 3.

**To Search on More Than One Drive:**

1. In the FileFind dialog box, select the **Entire Disk** option.
2. Pull down the Search menu and select the S**earch drives** option, or press **Alt-D**.
3. In the Drives to Search dialog box, select **All drives** to search all drives installed on your system, or select **The following drives:** and then select specific drives to search.

**To Narrow the Search:**

1.  Pull down the Search menu and select the **Advanced search** option, or press **F4**.

2.  In the Advanced Search dialog box, optionally specify a range of dates at the **Date is after:** and **Date is before:** prompts.

3.  Optionally specify a range of file sizes at the **Size is greater than:** and **Size is less than:** prompts.

4.  Optionally specify a file owner at the **Owner is:** prompt.

5.  Optionally select one of five toggle options: **File is Hidden**, **File is System File**, **File is Read-only**, **Archive bit is set**, and **Include Directories**.

These options narrow the search in that only files meeting *all conditions specified* in the Advanced Search dialog box are found (i.e., only files with dates, sizes, etc., in the specified range).

The Owner Is option in step 4 is for use on a network. It narrows the search to files belonging to one specific account or user.

The Hidden, System, Read-Only, and Archive toggles in step 5 narrow the search to those files with the indicated attributes set.

The Include Directories option may seem misplaced, as it actually expands the search. When set, FILEFIND finds directories, as well as files that match the file name to search for.

## To Go to a Specific File

1.  Highlight a file on the file list.
2.  In the FileFind dialog box, select **Go To**.

This command is unavailable until there is a file list in the FileFind dialog box (i.e., until you run a find or search).

Quitting FILEFIND by using the Quit! menu leaves you in the current default directory. The Go To option also quits the program but leaves you in the directory that contains the highlighted file (i.e., a new default directory).

## To Print the File List

1.   Pull down the List menu and select the P**rint list** option, or press **Ctrl-P**. The Print List dialog box appears.

2.   In the **Save the list to** box, choose a destination for printing: the printer or a file. If you choose a file, specify a file name at the **File:** prompt.

3.   In the Print List Format box, select how much file information you want to print.

4.   Optionally select any of the three toggle options available: **Print text search occurrences per file**, **Print directory totals**, and **Print totals for entire list**.

5.   Select **OK**.

This command is unavailable until there is a file list in the FileFind dialog box (i.e., until you run a find or search).

In step 2, if you print to a file, the default file name is filelist.bat. Though it is quite possible to create a batch file with this option, the Create Batch option is preferable, as it is more powerful. (See "To Create a Batch File.")

In step 3, there are five options. You can print only file names; file names and attributes; file names and sizes; file names, dates, and times; or file names, sizes, dates, and attributes (the default).

If you run a text search, toggle the Print Text Search Occurences Per File option on to print the number of matches found in each file, along with the selected file information.

Toggle the Print Directory Totals option on to print the number of files found in each listed directory and the amount of space they use.

Toggle the Print Totals for Entire List option on to print a grand total summing all directory totals (from previous option).

## To Quit FILEFIND

•   Select the Quit! menu.

See also "To Go to a Specific File."

## To Run a Target Fit

1. Pull down the Commands menu and select the **Target fit** option.

2. Select the target drive (install a floppy if necessary) and then select **OK**.

3. Select **OK** to acknowledge the results of the check.

Target Fit checks to see whether all the files on the current file list will fit on the target drive. This function was part of the FS (File Save) program in version 4.5 and is now completely contained within FILEFIND.

This function is only available when a file list appears in the File-Find dialog box (i.e., after you have run a find or search).

## To Search for Text

1. In the FileFind dialog box, enter the name of the file(s) in which to search for desired text at the **File Name:** prompt (wildcards and a path are OK).

2. At the **Containing:** prompt, type the text string for which you want to search.

3. Optionally choose a case-sensitive search by turning off the **Ignore case** toggle.

4. Specify the scope and the conditions of the search. (See "To Find a File or Files.")

5. In the FileFind dialog box, select **Start**.

6. Optionally view a file. (See "To View a File or Files.")

The TS (Text Search) program in version 4.5 has been incorporated into FILEFIND, though not completely. For example, although FILEFIND is capable of finding text within files, it is not able to do so on the erased portion of a disk.

In the resulting file list, the number of matches found in each file is displayed along with selected file information (see "To Configure the File List").

In step 1, specify the files in which FILEFIND is to search for text. To search all files in the designated scope, enter *.* after the prompt.

In step 3, the Ignore Case switch toggles case-sensitive searches on or off. If the switch is turned on (the default), the search is not case-sensitive. Searching for *Linda* will find every consecutive occurrence of the letters *l-i–n-d-a* without regard to case: *Linda, LINDA, LiNdA,* etc. If the switch is turned off, the search will find only exact matches of the search string. Searching for *Linda* will find only *Linda,* not *LINDA, linda, lInDa,* etc.

If, in step 6, you view a file you find, the search string will appear highlighted.

## To View a File or Files

1. Run a find or search. (See "To Find a File or Files.")

2. In the FileFind dialog box, highlight a file on the file list and select **View**.

3. To scroll the file, use the arrow keys or, if you have a mouse, use the scroll bar on the right side of the screen.

4. To view the next file in the list, pull down the Viewer menu and choose the **nExt file** option, or press **F8**.

5. To view the previous file in the list, pull down the Viewer menu and choose the **pRevious file** option, or press **F7**.

6. To see the next occurrence of the search string (if any) in the current file, pull down the Viewer menu and choose the N**ext match** option, or press **F6**.

7. To see the previous occurrence of the search string (if any) in the current file, pull down the Viewer menu and choose the P**revious match** option, or press **F5**.

8. When you are finished reading, pull down the Main! menu to return to the FileFind dialog box.

Omit steps 6 and 7 if you did not run a text search, as the Next Match and Previous Match commands will be unavailable.

FILEFIND's viewer only allows clear viewing of ASCII characters (viewed files cannot be edited). You can still view binary files but, as FILEFIND does not have a hex view, only ASCII characters can be read.

## ● SYNTAX

### FILEFIND (*filespec*) (*search string*) ( */options* )

*filespec* is the file(s) to find. In addition to standard DOS file-naming conventions (including wildcard use), FILEFIND also observes the following: .\*.* searches for every file in the current directory, and *:*.* searches for every file on every drive.

*search string* is the text to search for in a Text Search.

The options are the following:

**/A(+ ¦ –)** sets (+) or clears (–) the archive attribute for *filespec*.

**/BATCH** causes FILEFIND to exit to DOS when the search specified on the command line is finished. Use only with the /O:*filename* option.

**/C** searches for *filespec* in the current directory only. Equivalent to the Current Directory Only option.

**/CLEAR** clears all file attributes from *filespec*.

**/CS** performs a case-sensitive search. Equivalent to toggling the Ignore Case option off.

**/D(mm-dd-yy)** sets the file date for *filespec* to a specific month (*mm*), date (*dd*), and year (*yy*).

**/HID(+ ¦ –)** sets (+) or clears (–) the hidden attribute for *filespec*.

**/NOW** sets the file date and time for *filespec* to the current system time.

**/O:*filename*** prints the file list resulting from the search for the specified file.

**/R(+ ¦ –)** sets (+) or clears (–) the read-only attribute for *filespec*.

**/S** searches for *filespec* in the current directory and all its subdirectories. Equivalent to the Current Directory and Below option in the FileFind dialog box.

**/SYS(+ ¦ –)** sets (+) or clears (–) the system attribute for *filespec*.

**/T(hh:mm:ss)** sets the file time for *filespec* to a specific hour (*hh*), minute (*mm*), and second (*ss*).

**/TARGET:*drive*** performs a target fit—checks to see whether *filespec* will fit on the specified drive.

# FILEFIX

FILEFIX reconstructs new, error-free copies of damaged files. It repairs damaged spreadsheet files—those created with Lotus 1-2-3 and Symphony—and database files—those created with dBASE and Clipper.

● **UPGRADE INFORMATION**   FILEFIX is new to version 5.0 and has no predecessor in version 4.5.

## To Fix a Database File Automatically

1.  In the File Fix dialog box, select **dBASE**.

2.  In the Choose File to Repair dialog box, specify the name of the file you want to repair.

3.  In the Repair dBASE File dialog box, specify the name of the new, reconstructed file, select **Fully automatic** as the Repair Mode, specify the repair options, and then select **Begin**.

4.  Select **Skip Review**.

5.  Select the destination of the repair report—**Printer** or **File**—or select **No Report**.

6.  In the File Fix dialog box, select **Yes** to fix another file or select **No** to exit to DOS.

In step 2, specify the file you want to fix by typing its name at the **File name:** prompt or by selecting its name from the Drives, Dirs, and Files lists.

In step 3, you have three repair options: **Use Clipper field limits**, **Fix shifted data automatically**, and **Strict character checking**.

If you are repairing a Clipper file, turn on the first option. If you are repairing a dBASE file, turn it off.

In damaged database files, data may shift some number of spaces to the left or right across field boundaries. Turn on the second option to have FILEFIX fix this. In general, this option should be turned on.

The third option should almost always be turned on. Turn it off only if you have special graphics characters embedded in your fields. Such graphics are not produced with dBASE or Clipper but with a few third-party applications.

The damaged file is repaired automatically unless its header is corrupted. The file header contains information about the structure of the database (i.e., the number, name, size, type, etc., of component fields). If this is the case, the header must be manually repaired. This will occur after step 3. You may first be prompted to specify the version under which the damaged file was created; select **Revise Fields**, then follow the steps in the section "To Fix a Database File's Structure."

If you want to review or change header information, even though the header itself is undamaged, select **Review Fields** in step 4 instead of **Skip Review**.

## To Fix a Database File Manually

1. In the File Fix dialog box, select **dBASE**.
2. In the Choose File to Repair dialog box, specify the name of the file you want to repair.
3. In the Repair dBASE File dialog box, specify the name of the new, reconstructed file, select **Review damaged records** or **Review all records** as the Repair Mode, specify the repair options, and select **Begin**.
4. Select **Skip Review**.
5. For each record at which FILEFIX stops, select an action: **Accept, Reject, Shift,** or **Mode**.
6. Select the destination of the repair report—**Printer** or **File**— or select **No Report**.
7. In the File Fix dialog box, select **Yes** to fix another file or select **No** to exit to DOS.

In step 2, specify the file you want to fix by typing its name at the **File Name:** prompt or by selecting its name from the Drives, Dirs, and Files lists.

Database files can be manually repaired in two ways: You can choose to review every record or only those that are damaged.

Also in step 3, you have three repair options: **Use Clipper field limits**, **Fix shifted data automatically**, and **Strict character checking**. For an explanation of these options, see "To Fix a Database File Automatically."

If the file header (which contains information about the structure of the database) is damaged, you will be prompted to repair this after step 3. You may first be prompted to specify the version under which the damaged file was created; select **Revise Fields**, then follow the steps in the section "To Fix a Database File's Structure." When you are finished, you will return to step 4.

If you want to review or change header information, even though the header itself is undamaged, select **Review Fields** in step 4 instead of **Skip Review**.

In step 5, there are a number of options. For each record, select **Accept** to keep the record in its current state, and select **Reject** to discard the record. Select **Shift** and then press ← and → to properly align data within fields. When data is properly aligned, select **Done** and then **Accept**. Select **Mode** to change the Repair Mode.

## To Fix a Database File's Structure

1. In the Repair dBASE File dialog box, select **Review fields**.
2. Select **Revise**.
3. Select **Import**.
4. In the Choose Import File dialog box, specify the database containing the structure you want to import.
5. In the Repair dBASE File dialog box, select **Accept**.

or

1. In the Repair dBASE File dialog box, select **Review fields**.
2. Select **Revise**.
3. Select **Edit**.

4. Press ← or → until the data in the first field of the first record in the file sits next to the left edge of the on-screen box, and then select **OK**. This marks the beginning of file data.

5. Press ← or → until data is aligned in proper columns and then select **OK**. This establishes record size.

6. For each field displayed, press ← and → until data is correctly displayed within the field, select **Edit**, and specify the correct field name and type.

7. Once each field is finished, select **OK**.

8. Select **Accept**.

The structure of a database file can be fixed in one of three ways:

• Import the structure from another, healthy database file. To do this, use the first sequence of steps.

• Edit the structure manually. To do this, use the second sequence of steps.

• Import a similar but nonidentical structure from a healthy database and tailor it to a proper fit. To do this, use both sequences of steps, omitting step 4 from the first sequence.

## To Fix a Spreadsheet File

1. In the File Fix dialog box, select the kind of file you want to fix (1-2-3 or Symphony).

2. In the Choose File to Repair dialog box, specify the name of the file you want to fix.

3. In the Repair Spreadsheet File dialog box, specify the name of the new, reconstructed file, specify **Repair Mode**, and select **Begin**.

4. Select the destination of the repair report—**Printer** or **File**— or select **No Report**.

5. In the File Fix dialog box, select **Yes** to fix another file or select **No** to exit to DOS.

In step 2, specify the file you want to fix by typing its name at the **File Name:** prompt or by selecting its name from the Drives, Dirs, and Files lists.

In step 3, you can select one of two repair modes: **Attempt recovery of all data** and **Recover cell data only**. In almost all cases, it is possible to reconstruct an entire spreadsheet, so you should routinely choose the first option. If, however, damage to the file is particularly severe and complete recovery is not possible, choose the second option.

## ● SYNTAX

### FILEFIX (*filename.ext*)

When you indicate the file name and extension on the command line, FILEFIX senses whether you are working on a spreadsheet or on a database. Accordingly, it skips those steps where you enter the file type and name. Thus, in "To Fix a Spreadsheet File" and in "To Fix a Database File" (both automatically and manually), you begin at step 3.

● **NOTES**  FILEFIX works on files created by Lotus 1-2-3 versions 1, 1A, and 2, Symphony versions 1.0 and 1.1, and dBASE versions III, III+, and IV. One-hundred-percent-compatible files are also supported.

# FILESAVE

FILESAVE protects the data of specified files *after* deletion. Data from deleted files is held in a special subdirectory, virtually guaranteeing the successful unerasure of these files. Deleted files stored by FILESAVE are purged automatically after a specified number of days; you can purge them manually at any time.

● **UPGRADE INFORMATION**   FILESAVE is new to version 5.0 and has no predecessor in version 4.5.

## To Activate File Protection

1.  In the FileSave dialog box, select **Choose drives**.
2.  In the Choose Drives dialog box, select the drives to be protected and then select **ON**.
3.  Select **File protection** in the FileSave dialog box.
4.  In the File Protection dialog box, specify the files to be protected, the number of days you want to hold erased files, and the maximum amount of erased data you want to store.
5.  Select **OK**.
6.  Select **Quit** in the FileSave dialog box to return to the DOS prompt and save the settings.

Under DOS, when a file is erased, its entry is removed from its directory and the FAT, but its data remain on the disk. This makes unerasure possible. However, because the space used by the erased file is made available by DOS to new files, unerasure is not always successful; the erased file's data will eventually be overwritten. FILESAVE virtually guarantees successful unerasure of files by storing "erased" data in a special subdirectory called TRASHCAN. TRASHCAN and its contents are not overwritten by DOS unless TRASHCAN is the only place left on the disk to put new files.

In step 4, specifying files for protection involves a number of options (see Figure 5):

- You may protect all files on a disk, only files that you list, or all files except those that you list. File lists are compiled by extension (*.DOC, *.COM, etc.) in the Files list.

- Files that have been backed up through use of the DOS BACKUP program (i.e., those files with the Archive attribute turned off) will *not* be protected unless the **Include archived (backed up) files** option is turned on.

FILESAVE is a Terminate and Stay Resident (TSR) program that is loaded into memory when activated.

## To Deactivate File Protection

1. In the FileSave dialog box, select **Choose drives**.

2. Select **OFF** in the Choose Drives dialog box.

3. Select **Quit** in the FileSave dialog box to return to the DOS prompt.

FILESAVE is removed from memory when deactivated.

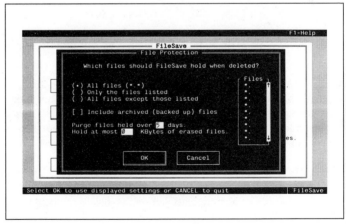

**Figure 5:** The File Protection dialog box

## To Purge Files (Manually)

1.  In the FileSave dialog box, select **Purge**.
2.  Optionally select a drive containing files to be purged: In the Purge Deleted Files dialog box, select **Drive**, then select the drive letter and **OK**.
3.  Mark the file or files you want to purge: Select **Tag** and enter the name of the file you want to mark in the Tag dialog box, or just double-click on the file(s) in the list.
4.  Select **Purge**.
5.  Select **Quit** in the FileSave dialog box to return to the DOS prompt.

## • SYNTAX

**FILESAVE (/** *options***)**

The options are the following:

**/ON** activates FILESAVE and loads it into memory.

**/OFF** deactivates FILESAVE and removes it from memory.

**/STATUS** displays current status and settings.

**/UNINSTALL** functions the same as /OFF.

# IMAGE

The IMAGE program protects your disks against accidental formatting. It saves essential disk information—the boot record, FAT, and root directory—to the file IMAGE.DAT. This file can then be used by UN-FORMAT to restore data to a formatted disk. (See UNFORMAT.)

IMAGE is one of the few programs in the Norton Utilities that does not have an interactive mode and can be used only from the command line.

● **UPGRADE INFORMATION**    IMAGE is essentially identical to the FR (Format Recover) /SAVE command in version 4.5. In fact, programs such as UNFORMAT that use the data file created by IMAGE (IMAGE.DAT) can also use the data file created by FR /SAVE (FRECOVER.DAT).

● **SYNTAX**

### IMAGE (*drive*:) (/NOBACK)

*drive*: specifies the drive for which IMAGE saves essential information. If *drive*: is omitted, the default drive is used.

**/NOBACK** causes IMAGE not to create the backup file IMAGE.BAK when it saves essential disk information.

● **NOTES**    IMAGE can protect both floppy disks and hard disks from accidental formats. However, only floppies formatted with Norton's Safe Format can be recovered. Floppies formatted with a DOS format cannot be recovered, as they are completely overwritten in the process (i.e., the IMAGE.DAT file, used to reconstruct the disk, is itself overwritten). Hard disks, by contrast, can almost always be unformatted, regardless of the formatting method. Hard-disk data is not overwritten during a format.

The file IMAGE.DAT *must* reside in the root directory in order for a disk to be properly unformatted. IMAGE automatically places IMAGE.DAT properly. Do not move this file.

# NCACHE-F, NCACHE-S

Caches speed up the operation of a computer by placing data recently read from disk in a memory buffer. When the data is needed again, it is read from memory, which is considerably faster than reading it from disk. Caches also place data to be written to disk in a buffer, speeding up operation by controlling exactly when disk writes occur.

The Norton Cache comes in two versions, NCACHE-F (Fast) and NCACHE-S (Small). NCACHE-F provides the greatest performance increase because of its intelligent reading and writing features (SmartReads and IntelliWrites); NCACHE-S should be used on systems with memory constraints (i.e., 640K or less of memory).

NCACHE is one of the few programs in the Norton Utilities 5.0 that does not have an interactive mode.

## ● UPGRADE INFORMATION   NCACHE is new to version 5.0 and has no predecessor in version 4.5.

## ● SYNTAX

### (DEVICE=*path*)NCACHE–(F ¦ S)(.EXE)(/*options*)

NCACHE can be loaded from the command line or from your CONFIG.SYS file as a device driver. If loaded as a device driver, **DEVICE=*path*** must begin the statement, where *path* specifies the location of NCACHE; the .EXE file extension must be appended. Options can also be specified in CONFIG.SYS. Neither DEVICE=*path* nor the .EXE extension are necessary when running NCACHE from the command line. (See the Appendix for information on CONFIG.SYS.)

The options that follow are for both NCACHE-F and NCACHE-S unless otherwise specified:

   **/(+ ¦ –)A** activates (+) or deactivates (–) the cache. Does not remove the cache from memory. (The default is +.)

**/BLOCK=*bytes*** specifies cache-block size. *Bytes* can equal 512, 1K, 2K, 4K, or 8K.

**/(+ ¦ –)C** activates (+) or deactivates (–) caching of additional data—that is, freezes cache contents when turned off (–). (The default is +.)

**DELAY=*secs.hths*** (NCACHE-F only) delays disk writes by the specified number of seconds and hundredths of a second. This speeds up disk-intensive applications. (The default is 0.0—off.)

**/DOS=(–)*bytes*** sizes the cache to *bytes* of conventional DOS memory. If *bytes* is preceded by a minus, the cache is sized to all available conventional DOS memory, minus *bytes*.

**/EXP=(–)*bytes*** sizes the cache to *bytes* of expanded memory. If *bytes* is preceded by a minus, the cache is sized to all available expanded memory, minus *bytes*. You can place some of the cache in conventional memory and some in expanded memory. You are not restricted to one or the other.

**/EXT=(–)*bytes*** sizes the cache to *bytes* of extended memory. If *bytes* is preceded by a minus, the cache is sized to all available extended memory, minus *bytes*. You can place some of the cache in conventional memory and some in extended memory. You are not restricted to one or the other.

**/F** flushes the contents of the cache.

**/G=*bytes*** sets the group sector size to the specified number of bytes. This sets the maximum amount of buffer space that any one data-read can occupy. (The default is 128K.)

**/HELP** displays the NCACHE help screen.

**/(+ ¦ –)I** (NCACHE-F only) activates (+) or deactivates (–) intelligent disk writes (IntelliWrites). Speeds up operation by writing to disk while control has returned to the current application, rather than by returning control after the disk write is complete.

**/INI=*path*** specifies the location of the NCACHE configuration file NCACHE.INI. This file is created with the /SAVE option.

**/PRINT** prints the NCACHE status screen.

**/QUICK=ON ¦ OFF** (NCACHE-F only) activates (ON) or deactivates (OFF) quick prompts. Use with the /I (IntelliWrites) option. Speeds up operation by returning to DOS before all disk writes are complete.

**/R=(D)***sectors* (NCACHE-F only) causes NCACHE to read ahead the specified sectors. Speeds up operation by reading into the cache the next most likely group of sectors, before they are actually requested by the application. Adding the D prefix (dynamic read-ahead) enables reading ahead only when probable sectors are sitting sequentially on the disk.

**/RESET** resets the cache to its newly loaded state. Similar to /F.

**/(+ ¦ –)S** (NCACHE-F only) activates (+) or deactivates (–) SmartReads. Speeds up operation by executing all reads before all writes.

**/SAVE** saves the current configuration to the file NCACHE.INI.

**/STATUS** displays the NCACHE status screen.

**/UNINSTALL** removes NCACHE from memory. It cannot be removed if it was loaded as a device in CONFIG.SYS; it can only be removed if it was the last Terminate and Stay Resident (TSR) program loaded.

**/USEHIDOS=(Y ¦ N)**, if set to Y, loads the NCACHE program itself (as opposed to the actual cache) into high DOS memory. This is only possible when extended or expanded memory drivers are loaded.

**/USEHMA=(Y ¦ N)**, if set to Y, loads the NCACHE program itself (as opposed to the actual cache) into extended memory.

**/(+ ¦ -)W** activates (+) or deactivates (–) Write-through. Speeds up operation by caching disk writes as well as disk reads. It has no effect when /I (IntelliWrites) is on.

● **NOTES**   Do not use the DOS program FASTOPEN with NCACHE, as NCACHE takes over its functions.

# NCC
## Norton Control Center

NCC gives you control over a number of system options and settings: cursor size; text, background, border, and palette colors; video mode; keyboard repeat rate; mouse sensitivity; serial port configuration; and system date and time. It also provides four stopwatches.

● **UPGRADE INFORMATION**  The Norton Control Center in version 5.0 is slightly expanded from the one in version 4.5. Control over mouse sensitivity and country information (international dates, times, and currency formats) and the ability to save settings to a file have been added. In addition, the Time Mark (TM) program (which is not a stand-alone program in version 5.0) has been incorporated into NCC.

## To Change Cursor Size

   1.  In the Select Item box, select C**ursor Size.**
   2.  In the Cursor Size box, adjust the size of the cursor by repositioning the Start and End arrows. (See Figure 6.)
   3.  Select **OK**.

The Start and End arrows can be adjusted with ↑ and ↓ or by dragging with the mouse. (You can select the arrows with ← and → if you don't have a mouse.) Make certain that the Start arrow is above the End arrow; otherwise, your cursor is likely to disappear.

The results of adjusting cursor size are at all times previewed in the Cursor Size box under the Actual Size prompt.

In step 2, you can return the cursor to its default size by selecting **Default** in the Cursor Size box.

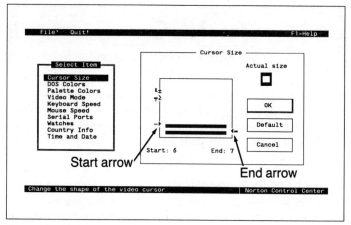

**Start arrow** / **End arrow**

**Figure 6:** The Start and End arrows

## To Change DOS Colors (Text, Background, and Border)

1. In the Select Item box, select D**OS Colors.**

2. In the DOS Colors box and in the Text Color box, select the DOS text color and background color.

3. In the Border Color box, select a border color.

4. In the Background box, select whether background colors should be **Bright** or **Blinking.**

5. Select **OK**.

If you are going to use the DOS Colors function, you should load the ANSI.SYS driver in your CONFIG.SYS file (see the Appendix if you need help with this). Although this is not necessary, the color changes you make are less likely to be undone by programs that themselves set text and background colors.

In step 2, the text color and background color are set in combination; that is, all possible combinations of text and background colors are available in the Text Color box.

The default colors can be reset by selecting the **Default** option in the DOS Colors box.

## To Change Palette Colors

1.  In the Select Item box, select **Palette Colors**.

2.  In the Palette Colors box, use the pointer arrows to indicate the color you want to change.

3.  Select the **Change** option.

4.  In the Change Color dialog box, select a new color and then select **OK**.

5.  Repeat steps 2–4 for each color you want to change.

6.  In the Palette Colors box, select **OK** when finished.

This function is available only if you have a monitor with EGA or VGA graphics.

To return an individual color to its default setting, choose the **Default** option in the Change Color dialog box in step 4.

To return all colors to their default settings, choose the **Default** option in the Palette Colors box.


## To Change the Selected Country

1.  To change the selected country and country information, choose **Country Info** in the Select Item box.

2.  In the Country Info box, highlight the country whose formats you want to use and select **OK**.

This function is only available if the COUNTRY parameter has been set in your CONFIG.SYS file or the NLSFUNC program has been run. See your DOS manual for details.

In step 2, when you select a new country, the Time, Date, Currency, List, and Numbers formats change accordingly.


## To Change System Date and Time

1.  In the Select Item box, select **Time and Date**. The Time and Date box appears.

2.  In the Date box, highlight the month, date, and year; use the plus (+) key to change the values upward, and the

minus (−) key to change them downward. (Use the plus and minus keys on the numeric keypad, not the main keyboard.)

3. In the Time box, highlight the hour, minutes, and seconds; use the plus key to change the values upward, and the minus key to change them downward.

4. Select **OK**.

On computers where the system configuration is stored in CMOS, this function changes the CMOS date and time, thereby making the changes permanent. On computers that have only a clock/calendar or nothing at all, the date and time are changed for the current session only. After rebooting or powering up, the date and time have to be reset.

## To Change the Video Mode

1. In the Select Item box, select **Video Mode.**

2. In the Video Mode box and in the Display Lines box, select the number of lines of text to display on the screen.

3. In the Display Mode box, select either the **Black and White** option or the **Color** option.

4. Select **OK**.

The options available to you with the Video Mode function depend entirely on the kind of video card installed in your system. In step 2, the option to change the number of display lines is only available if you have an EGA- or VGA-equipped system. Neither the Display Lines option nor the Display Mode options are available on a system with monochrome graphics (Hercules and compatible graphics).

## To Configure Serial Ports

1. In the Select Item box, select **Serial Ports.**

2. At the top of the Serial Ports box, highlight the port to be configured.

3. In the Baud box, select the rate at which the serial port communicates.

**4.** In the Parity box, select the parity setting at which the serial port communicates.

**5.** In the Data Bits box, select the number of data bits in each byte transmitted.

**6.** In the Stop Bits box, select the number of stop bits to be sent after each byte of data sent.

**7.** Repeat steps 2–6 for each port.

**8.** Select **OK**.

In order for your computer to communicate via a serial port with any external device (mouse, laser printer, modem, etc.), the serial port must be properly configured. The port and the external device must use the same protocols and settings (whatever those may be; it is entirely dependent on the particular situation).

## To Restore Saved Settings

**1.** Pull down the File menu and select the **Load settings** option, or press **F3**.

**2.** In the Load Settings dialog box, enter the name of the file that contains the settings you want to load and then select **OK**.

## To Save NCC Settings to a File

**1.** Pull down the File menu and select the **Save settings** option, or press **F2**. The Save Settings dialog box appears.

**2.** In the Settings box, specify the settings to be saved.

**3.** In the File Name box, type the name of the file that will contain the saved settings.

**4.** Select **OK**.

Settings that are saved in a file can be implemented simultaneously. You do not have to reset everything each time you use your computer. (See "To Restore Saved Settings.")

## To Set the Keyboard Repeat Rate

**1.** In the Select Item box, select **Keyboard Speed**.

2. In the Keyboard Speed box, set the keyboard repeat rate by moving the top "belt buckle" left or right.

3. Set the repeat delay by moving the second "belt buckle" left or right.

4. Optionally hold down a key to test the new settings. Results are visible at the Keyboard Test Pad prompt.

5. Select **OK**.

The *keyboard repeat rate* is the rate at which a character is repeated on the screen when a key is depressed and held down. It can be set as slow as 2 characters per second and as fast as 30 characters per second. The keyboard repeat rate can be set on all 286, 386, and 486 computers and on some 8088 and 8086 computers.

The *repeat delay* is the length of time a key must be held down before a character is repeated. It can be set as slow as 1 second and as fast as 0.25 seconds and works on 286, 386, and 486 computers.

In steps 2 and 3, "belt buckles" can be moved with the ←, →, Home, and End keys or by dragging the mouse.

Repeat rate and delay can be set automatically to their fastest settings by selecting **Fast** in the Keyboard Speed box.

## To Set Mouse Sensitivity

1. In the Select Item box, select M**ouse Speed.**

2. In the Mouse Speed box, move the "belt buckle" to adjust mouse sensitivity.

3. Optionally move your mouse to test the new settings.

4. Select **OK**.

In step 2, the "belt buckle" can be moved with the ←, →, Home, and End keys or by dragging the mouse.

Mouse sensitivity can be returned to its default setting by selecting the **Default** option in the Mouse Speed box.

## To Use Stopwatches/Timers

1. In the Select Item box, select W**atches.**

**2.**   In the Watches box, select any of four watches you want to use.

**3.**   Select **Start** to start the watch, **Pause** to stop it, or **Reset** to reset it to zero.

The Time Mark (TM) program in version 4.5 is incorporated into NCC. When you first start a watch, the current system time is displayed.

## ● SYNTAX

**NCC (*filename*) (/SET)**

or

**NCC (/*options*)**

*filename* specifies the file containing saved NCC settings. If *filename* is specified, the **/SET** option must be used to load the settings.

The options are the following:

**/25** sets number of display lines to 25.

**/35** sets number of display lines to 35 (EGA only).

**/40** sets number of display lines to 40 (VGA only).

**/43** sets number of display lines to 43 (EGA only).

**/50** sets number of display lines to 50 (VGA only).

**/BW80** sets display to black and white, 80 columns, 25 rows.

**/c:*comment*** displays *comment*. Comments that include spaces must be enclosed in quotation marks.

**/CO80** sets display to color, 80 columns, 25 rows.

**/FAST** sets keyboard repeat rate and delay to the fastest settings.

**/L** displays current time and date on the left side of screen.

**/N** suppresses display of current time and date.

**/START:** # starts the stopwatch with the specified number. If # is omitted, watch number 1 is started.

**/STOP:** # stops the stopwatch with the specified number. If # is omitted, watch number 1 is stopped.

# NCD

## Norton Change Directory

NCD is a subdirectory manager. It lets you create, delete, and rename subdirectories, as well as navigate easily among them.

● **UPGRADE INFORMATION**   NCD in version 5.0 is essentially the same as NCD in version 4.5, though slightly expanded—it also contains the functions of the Volume Label (VL) and List Directories (LD) programs.

## To Change Directories

1. Highlight the directory that you want to change to.
2. Press ↵.

In step 1, highlight the target directory by using ↑ and ↓ or the built-in Speed Search function. To use Speed Search, simply type the first letter or letters of the directory you want to highlight. Each time you type a letter, the highlight bar jumps to the next directory name beginning with the letter typed. Pressing Ctrl-↵ cycles the highlight bar through all directories that match the current search string.

## To Change Drives

1. Pull down the Disk menu and select the **Change disk** option, or press **F3**.
2. In the dialog box that appears, select a new drive.

## To Change the Number of Display Lines

1. Pull down the View menu.
2. Select the number of lines to display on-screen.

This function is only available if you have EGA or VGA graphics.

The choices available in step 2 are determined by the kind of graphics card you have. A VGA card supports 25, 40, and 50 lines; EGA supports 25, 35, and 43.

This function changes the display for the NCD program only. If you want to change the display lines systemwide, use the NCC program (see NCC, "To Change the Video Mode").

## To Change or Delete a Volume Label

1. Pull down the Disk menu and select the V**olume label** option, or press **Alt-V**.

2. In the Volume Label dialog box, type the new volume label and select **OK**.

To delete a drive's volume label, select the D**elete** option in the Volume Label dialog box in step 2.

## To Delete a Directory

1. Highlight the directory you want to delete.

2. Pull down the Directory menu and select the D**elete** option, or press **F8**.

3. If the directory contains files, review the file list in the caution box and select **Yes** to proceed with the deletion.

Files contained within a directory are deleted if the directory is deleted.

## To Make a Directory

1. Highlight the directory that will contain the new directory (i.e., highlight the parent-to-be directory).

2. Pull down the Directory menu and select the M**ake** option, or press **F7**.

3. In the dialog box that appears, enter the name of the directory you want to create and select **OK**.

In step 1, highlight the directory by using the arrow keys or Speed Search. (See "To Change a Directory" for an explanation.)

## To Print the Directory Tree

1.  Pull down the Directory menu and select the P**rint tree** option, or press **Alt-P**.

2.  In the Print Tree dialog box and at the **Print the Directory Structure to:** prompt, specify where the tree is to be printed.

3.  In the Tree Format box, specify the format with which the tree is to be printed.

4.  Select **Print**.

Trees can be printed to a printer or a file, so in step 1, specify either a file name or the device to which a printer is attached (PRN, lpt1:, lpt2:, etc.). If you print a tree to a file, there is an added step: Select **OK** to acknowledge the creation of a new file.

In step 3, there are three possible tree formats:

*   Select **Tree, Graphic chars** to print the tree as it appears on-screen: directory names connected by lines.

*   Select **Tree, Non-graphic chars** if your printer is unable to print graphics. This prints a tree with hyphens, plus signs, etc.

*   Select **List** to get a simple list of directories not in tree format.

## To Quit NCD

*   Select the Quit! menu, or press **Esc**.

## To Rename a Directory

1.  Highlight the directory you want to rename.

2.  Pull down the Directory menu and select the R**ename** option, or press **F6**.

3.  In the dialog box that appears, type the new directory name and select **OK**.

In step 1, highlight the directory by using the arrow keys or Speed Search. (See "To Change a Directory" for an explanation.)

This function is unavailable if you are using a DOS version prior to 3.0.

## To Rescan a Disk

1. Pull down the Disk menu and select the **Rescan disk** option, or press **F2**.

2. In the Rescan Disk dialog box, select **Yes**.

When NCD is run on a drive for the first time, it stores directory information in a file named TREEINFO.NCD (though this file will not be created on drives with five or fewer directories). In subsequent uses of the program, NCD reads directory information from this file rather than rescanning the drive, which saves you some time. Changes made to the directory tree (for example, renaming, adding, or deleting a directory) with NCD are reflected automatically in TREEINFO.NCD. Changes made with DOS or some other utility are not. If, then, you make a change to a directory and run NCD, the directory tree displayed is not accurate. You have to rescan the disk to put current information in TREEINFO.NCD.

● SYNTAX

### NCD (MD : RD) dir: (/*options*)

*dir* is the name of the directory you want to make (NCD MD *dir*), remove (NCD RD *dir*), or change to. If you are changing to a directory, only the lowest-level directory in the target path has to be specified (for example, *DOCS* for \WP\WORD\DOCS).

The options are the following:

**/N** causes NCD not to update TREEINFO.NCD during operation.

**/R** rescans the disk and updates TREEINFO.NCD (see "To Rescan a Directory").

**/V:***label* attaches the specified volume label to the disk.

● **NOTES**   The TREEINFO.NCD file is placed in the root directory of a drive. If you move it, NCD will be unable to locate it and will rescan the disk and re-create the file.

**See Also**   DISKEDIT

# NDD

## Norton Disk Doctor II

NDD checks for and repairs errors in the system area—specifically, the partition table, boot record, directory tree, and file allocation table (FAT)—and errors on the disk medium itself (i.e., physically damaged sectors).

● **UPGRADE INFORMATION** The Norton Disk Doctor II is very similar to the Norton Disk Doctor I in version 4.5. There are, however, two distinct differences:

- The Solutions to Common Problems function in NDD I (version 4.5) has been moved to the DISKTOOL program in version 5.0.

- NDD II contains the Disk Test (DT) program that is in version 4.5.

## To Configure NDD

1. In the Norton Disk Doctor II dialog box, select **Options**.
2. Select one of the configuration sequences below (set surface test options, set a custom error message, or skip certain tests).
3. In the Disk Doctor Options dialog box, select **OK** to set these options for the current NDD session only, or select **Save Settings** to set options for both current and future sessions.

### To Set Surface Test Options:

1. In the Disk Doctor Options dialog box, select **Surface Test**.
2. Set surface test options exactly as in steps 7–10 in "To Test (and Repair) a Disk."

### To Set a Custom Error Message:

1. In the Disk Doctor Options dialog box, select **Custom Message**.

2. In the Set Custom Message dialog box, toggle the **Prompt with Custom Message** option on.

3. Press **F2** to select a text attribute for the message.

4. Type the message in the message square.

5. Select **OK**.

Using a custom message prevents NDD from correcting system area errors (i.e., errors in the FAT, directory structure, boot record, etc.) and makes steps 4 and 5 in "To Test (and Repair) a Disk" unnecessary.

In step 3, there are four text attributes from which to choose: normal, bold, underline, and reverse. The text you type appears in whatever attribute is selected. You can, therefore, produce messages with multiple attributes by repeating steps 3 and 4 for different parts of the message.

**To Skip Certain Tests:**

1. In the Disk Doctor Options dialog box, select **Tests to Skip**.

2. In the Tests to Skip dialog box, select the test or tests you want to skip.

3. Select **OK**.

In step 2, there are four tests you can have NDD skip:

- Select **Skip Partition Tests** to omit testing of the integrity of the partition table on your hard disk. Some proprietary partitioning software may cause NDD difficulty.

- Select **Skip CMOS Tests** to omit testing of your machine's CMOS (where date, time, and configuration information is stored).

- Select **Skip Surface Tests** to omit testing of your disk for physical errors. Selecting this option automatically skips steps 7–11 in "To Test (and Repair) a Disk."

- Select **Only 1 Hard Disk** if your computer has only one physical hard-disk drive installed but NDD reports more than one.

## To Quit NDD

- In the Norton Disk Doctor II dialog box, select **Quit Disk Doctor** or press **Esc**.

## To Test (and Repair) a Disk

1. In the Norton Disk Doctor II dialog box, select **Diagnose Disk**.
2. In the Select Drives to Diagnose dialog box, select the disk or disks you want to test, and then select **Diagnose**.
3. If errors are found, read the explanation box(es) and select **Continue**.
4. When prompted to correct errors, select **Yes** to correct them or **No** to let them alone.
5. Follow any prompts NDD presents to correct errors.
6. In the Create UNDO File dialog box, select the drive on which you want to store the Undo file, or select **Cancel** to skip this step.
7. In the Surface Test dialog box and in the Test box, select whether you want NDD to test the entire surface of the disk for damage or just the space occupied by files.
8. In the Test Type box, select the surface test depth (how thoroughly NDD tests the disk surface).
9. In the Passes box, select how many times you want NDD to perform the surface test.
10. In the Repair Setting box, select a repair option.
11. Select **Begin Test**.
12. On the summary screen, optionally print a report of NDD findings and actions by selecting **Report**.
13. On the Report for Drive screen, select **Print** to print the NDD report, or select **Save as** to save it in a file. If you choose **Save as**, enter the name of the report file in the Save Report dialog box.
14. Select **Done**.

In step 2, select the drives you want to diagnose by highlighting them and pressing the spacebar or by clicking on them once with the mouse.

If you select No in step 4, NDD does not correct the errors it has found, and you skip to step 7.

In step 5, the actual dialog boxes you see depend on the errors found.

In step 6, you create a file that allows you to undo NDD's corrections. (See "To Undo NDD Corrections.")

Steps 7 through 11 constitute the surface test (the same as the Disk Test (DT) program in version 4.5), which checks for physical errors on a disk. If you want to skip these steps, select **Cancel** in step 7 and go to step 12. Otherwise, in step 7, select **Disk Test** to have NDD test the entire disk surface for physical errors, or select **File Test** to have it test only the areas of the disk with data on them (i.e., files).

In step 8, there are three types of tests:

- Select **Daily** to have NDD perform a "light" test.

- Select **Weekly** to have NDD perform a more thorough (and longer) test.

- Select **Auto Weekly** (the default) if you are going to use NDD every day for preventive maintenance. This option causes NDD to perform a Daily test on every day of the week (as determined by your system clock), except Friday when it performs a Weekly test.

In step 9, select **Repetitions** to specify exactly how many times the surface test is to be done. Select **Continuous** to run the surface test until you interrupt it.

In step 10, you set the repair options for the surface test, not the system area test that occurs in steps 2 through 5.

- Select **Don't Repair** if you want to leave any surface errors NDD finds.

- Select **Prompt before Repairing** to have NDD prompt you before it fixes a surface error.

- Select **Repair Automatically** to have NDD fix any errors it finds without prompting you first.

## To Undo NDD Corrections

1. In the Norton Disk Doctor II dialog box, select **Undo Changes**.
2. In the Undo Changes dialog box, select **Yes**.
3. Select the drive containing the Undo file.
4. Select **OK** in the confirmation box.
5. Select **OK** to acknowledge completion of the operation.

This function allows you to undo the changes or corrections made with NDD. To undo NDD corrections, however, you must have saved an Undo file in step 6 of "To Test (and Repair) a Disk."

The Undo file is always called NDDUNDO.DAT.

## ● SYNTAX

NDD (*drive*:) (*drive*:) (/*options*)

*drive*: specifies the drive(s) to test and repair.

The options are the following:

**/COMPLETE** tests the system area and performs a surface test on the indicated drive(s).

**/QUICK** tests the system area but does not perform a surface test.

**/R:***filename* sends a report to the specified file. Use this option with /QUICK or /COMPLETE.

**/RA:***filename* appends a report to the specified file. Use this option with /QUICK and /COMPLETE.

**/REBUILD** has NDD attempt to reconstruct a critically damaged disk.

**/UNDELETE** undeletes a partition.

**/X:*drive*** excludes the specified drive from testing. Excluded drives do not appear for selection in the Select Drives to Diagnose dialog box.

**See Also**    DISKTOOL

# NORTON
## Norton Utilities Shell

The NORTON program is a shell from which you can run any of the programs that comprise the Norton Utilities or any other frequently used program. NORTON also provides explanations for common errors and the ability to configure the Norton Utilities.

● **UPGRADE INFORMATION**   NORTON is an expanded version of the Norton Integrator (NI) in version 4.5.

## To Add a Program (or Command) to the Program List

1. Pull down the Configure menu, and select the **Add menu item** option.
2. In the Add Menu Item box, select **Command**.
3. At the **Name in menu:** prompt, type the program (or command) name as you want it to appear in the program list.
4. At the **DOS command:** prompt, type the DOS command that runs the program (or that is the command in question). Include a path if necessary.
5. In the Topic box, select the topic under which the program (or command) should be listed when the program list is sorted by topic.
6. Select **Description**.
7. Press **F2** to select a text attribute for the description.
8. In the Description box, type a description of the program (or command).
9. Select **OK** twice.

This function allows you to run any program (or execute any command) from NORTON.

In step 7, there are four text attributes from which to choose: normal, bold, underline, and reverse. The text you type appears in whatever attribute is selected. You can, therefore, produce descriptions with multiple attributes by repeating steps 7 and 8 for different parts of the description.

When the program list is sorted by name, step 2 is omitted.

## To Add a Topic to the Program List

1. Sort the program list by topic. (See "To Sort the Program List.")
2. Pull down the Configure menu, and select the **Add menu item** option.
3. In the Add Menu Item dialog box, select **Topic**.
4. Type the name of the new topic.
5. Select **Description**.
6. Press **F2** to select a text attribute for the description.
7. In the Description box, type a description of the topic.
8. Select **OK** twice.

This function is only possible when the program list is sorted by topic. (You can have as many as ten topics.)

In step 6, there are four text attributes from which to choose: normal, bold, underline, and reverse. The text you type appears in whatever attribute is selected. You can, therefore, produce descriptions with multiple attributes by repeating steps 6 and 7 for different parts of the description.

## To Configure the Norton Utilities

1. Pull down the Configure menu, and select **Video and mouse options.**
2. In the Video and Mouse Options dialog box and in the Screen Colors box, select a color mode.
3. In the Screen Options box, specify box and background options.
4. In the Graphics Options box, select a graphics mode.

**5.** In the Mouse Options box, select the desired mouse options.

**6.** Select **Save**.

In step 2, there are five available color modes:

- Select **Laptop** if you are using a laptop computer.
- Select **Black and White** if you are using a composite monitor.
- Select **Monochrome** if you are using a monochrome monitor.
- Select **Color** or **Alternate Color** if you are using a color monitor.

In step 3, toggle **Zooming boxes** on to have dialog boxes "explode," or expand, from their centers when drawn. Toggle **Solid background** on or off to switch between a solid background and a tessellated background.

In step 4, the graphics options control the appearance of the mouse pointer, buttons, toggle boxes, and check marks:

- Select **Graphical controls and mouse pointer** to provide an arrow for the mouse pointer, complete circles for buttons, complete squares for toggle boxes, and check marks to indicate that an option is toggled on.
- Select **Graphical controls** to provide all of the above, except the arrow for the mouse pointer (which becomes a block).
- Select **Standard** to draw all these options as ASCII characters instead of as graphics. The mouse pointer is a block, buttons are parentheses, toggle boxes are square brackets, and check marks are $X$'s.

The two graphical options are only available if you have an EGA or VGA video display card.

In step 5, select **Left-handed mouse** to reverse the functions of the mouse buttons. Select **Fast mouse reset** for automatic, proper positioning of the mouse pointer and the most efficient use of the Norton Utilities.

## To Delete a Program or
## Topic from the Program List

1. In the Norton Utilities 5.0 dialog box and in the Commands box (program list), highlight the program or topic you want to delete.

2. Pull down the Configure menu, and select the **Delete menu item** option.

3. In the Delete Menu Item dialog box, select **Yes** to confirm the deletion.

To delete a topic, the program list must be sorted by topic. Programs (or commands) can be deleted regardless of sort order.

A topic cannot be deleted if it has programs (or commands) listed beneath it.

## To Edit a Program Entry on the Program List

1. Highlight the program (or command) you want to edit.

2. Pull down the Configure menu, and select the **Edit menu item** option.

3. Follow steps 3–9 in "To Add a Program (or Command) to the Program List," changing the current information as you go.

## To Edit a Topic Entry on the Program List

1. Highlight the topic you want to edit.

2. Pull down the Configure menu, and select the **Edit menu item** option.

3. Follow steps 4–8 in "To Add a Topic to the Program List," changing the current information as you go.

## To Get Solutions to Common Problems

1. Pull down the Advise menu, and select the **common disk Problems** option.

2. In the Common Disk Problems dialog box and at the **Problem:** prompt, highlight the problem that you want to solve.
3. Select **Expand**.
4. Select **Done** when finished, or, if it is available, select the option to run the appropriate remedying program.

In step 4, since the Norton Utilities can fix many common problems, you will occasionally have the option to run a program that will fix the problem.

## To Quit NORTON

• Select the Quit! menu, or press **Esc**.

## To Run a Program (or Command) from NORTON

1. In the Norton Utilities 5.0 dialog box and in the Commands box (program list), highlight the name of the program you want to run.
2. On the command line at the cursor, next to where the name of the program to run appears, type any required arguments or switches.
3. Press ↵.

## To Sort the Program List

1. Pull down the Configure menu.
2. Choose the **sort by Name** option or press **Alt-N** to sort the list by program name. Choose **sort by Topic** or press **Alt-T** to sort by topic.

## To View CHKDSK Error Messages, Explanations, Solutions

1. Pull down the Advise menu, and select the **CHKDSK error messages** option.

2. In the CHKDSK Error Messages dialog box, highlight the error message in question.

3. Select **Expand**.

4. Select **Done** when you are finished reading, or, if it is available, select the option to run the appropriate remedying program.

In step 4, you will occasionally have the option to run a program that will correct the error.

## To View DOS Error Messages, Explanations, Solutions

1. Pull down the Advise menu, and select the **DOS error messages** option.

2. In the DOS Error Messages dialog box, highlight the error message in question.

3. Select **Expand**.

4. Select **Done** when you are finished reading, or, if it is available, select the option to run the appropriate remedying program.

In step 4, you will occasionally have the option to run a program that will correct the error.

● **SYNTAX**

**NORTON (/***options***)**

The options are the following:

**/BW** specifies use of the Black and White mode. For use with composite monitors.

**/G0** specifies use of the Standard graphics option. (See "To Configure the Norton Utilities," step 4.) EGA and VGA only.

**/G1** specifies use of the Graphical Controls graphics option. (See "To Configure the Norton Utilities," step 4.) EGA and VGA only.

**/LCD** specifies use of the Laptop color mode. For use with LCD displays.

**/NOZOOM** tells Norton not to use exploding dialog boxes. (See "To Configure the Norton Utilities," step 3.)

# SFORMAT
## *Safe Format*

SFORMAT is better than the FORMAT program in DOS, as it is able to format disks more quickly and in such a way that they can be unformatted without data loss.

● **UPGRADE INFORMATION** SFORMAT is essentially the same as the Safe Format (SF) program in version 4.5.

## To Allow or Disallow Formatting of Hard Disks

1. Pull down the Configure menu and select the H**ard disks** option, or press **Alt-H**.

2. In the Hard Disk Formatting box, toggle the A**llow Hard Disk Formatting** option on or off, and select **OK**.

To prevent accidental formatting of hard disks, this option is turned off by default.

## To Format a Disk

1. In the Safe Format dialog box and in the Drive box, select the drive you want to format.

2. If you are formatting a floppy, select the desired disk capacity in the Size box.

3. In the System Files box, choose what you want to do with the DOS system files.

4. In the Format Mode box, choose what kind of format you want to execute.

5. At the **Volume Label:** prompt, type the volume label you want to assign to the formatted disk, if any.

6. Optionally toggle the **Save IMAGE Info** option on.

7. Select **Begin Format**.

8. Select **Yes** if a confirmation box appears.

In step 2, the sizes you can choose from depend on the types of drives you have. Five-and-a-quarter-inch drives can be formatted to 1.2Mb, 360K, 320K, 180K, and 160K. Three-and-a-half-inch drives can be formatted to 1.44Mb and 720K. This option is not available if you are formatting a hard disk.

In step 3, you have three options:

- Select **Don't put on disk** if you do not want to format a bootable disk.

- Select **Put on disk** if you want to format a bootable disk.

- Select **Leave space** if you are undecided. This option allows you to add the system files subsequently with the SYS command in DOS.

In step 4, you have three options:

- Select **Safe** to perform a safe format, which allows you to unformat the disk and recover any data on it, if necessary.

- Select **Quick** to perform the fastest format. This effectively blanks the disk by overwriting system information (directory structure, boot record, FAT).

- Select **DOS** to perform a normal DOS format.

In step 6, the Save IMAGE Info option must be toggled on if you are doing a safe format. IMAGE information allows a formatted disk to be recovered with the UNFORMAT program. (See IMAGE and UNFORMAT.)

## To Save Current Settings

- Pull down the Configure menu, and select the S**ave settings** option.

## To Set Default Floppy Types

1. Pull down the Configure menu and select the F**loppy Types** option. The Floppy Types dialog box appears.

2. In the Floppy Drives box, select the drive whose default type you want to set.

3.  In the Type for Drive box, specify the default floppy type and size.

4.  Select **OK**.

5.  Save your settings. (See "To Save Current Settings.")

Use this function if, for example, you frequently format 360K disks in a 1.2Mb drive.

## ● SYNTAX

**SFORMAT (***drive***:) (/***options***)**

*drive*: is the drive you want to format or the target drive.

The options are the following:

**/1** formats a single-sided disk.

**/4** formats a double-density (360K) disk in a high-density (1.2Mb) disk drive.

**/8** formats the target disk with 8 sectors per track instead of the usual 9.

**/A** formats the target drive automatically, using current or default settings, and quits to DOS.

**/B** formats the target drive, leaving space for the DOS system files. Allows you subsequently to make the disk bootable with the SYS command in DOS.

**/***bytes* specifies the formatted size of the target disk. Equivalent to selecting a size in step 2 of "To Format a Disk." Entering **/360**, for example, formats a 360K disk.

**/D** performs a normal DOS format.

**/N:#** specifies the number of sectors per track; # can equal 8, 9, 15, or 18.

**/Q** performs a quick format.

**/S** makes the target drive bootable.

**/T:#** specifies the number of tracks to be written on the disk; # can equal 40 or 80.

**/V:***label* attaches the specified volume label to the formatted drive.

● **NOTES**   During installation of the Norton Utilities, you have the option to rename the DOS FORMAT program XXFORMAT and to rename the SFORMAT program FORMAT.

**See Also**   IMAGE, UNFORMAT

# SPEEDISK
## The Disk Defragmentation Program

When DOS writes a file to disk, the first cluster in the file is placed in the first available cluster on disk, the next cluster in the file is placed in the next available cluster, and so on, filling the disk from front to back. As a result, when files are copied onto an empty hard disk, each file's clusters sit together in one area of the disk.

After much use, however, a file's clusters can be scattered over different areas of the disk. For example, if a 20K file is deleted and a 25K file is written to the disk, the first 20K of the new file fits into the vacated space, while the remaining 5K must be placed elsewhere. Although this is simply a result of normal DOS bookkeeping, a hard disk with files scattered all over will noticeably slow down your computer. The read-write heads must travel the entire surface of the disk just to find one file.

Finding a file is much faster if its component clusters are consecutive. SPEEDISK optimizes, or defragments, your hard disk, placing the clusters of each file next to one another and moving all files toward the beginning of the disk.

● **UPGRADE INFORMATION** SPEEDISK is an expanded version of the SD (Speed Disk) program in version 4.5 and can perform the functions of DS (Directory Sort) as well.

## To Defragment/Optimize a Hard Disk

1. Start SPEEDISK.
2. In the dialog box that appears, select the drive you want to defragment.
3. In the Recommendation dialog box, select **Optimize** to run SPEEDISK as it is currently configured, or select **Configure** to reconfigure the program. If you select Optimize, skip to step 12. If you select Configure, continue with steps 4 through 11.

4. Optionally specify the order in which directories are written to disk during optimization. (See "To Specify Directory Order.")

5. Optionally specify the order in which files are to be listed within directories. (See "To Sort Files within Directories.")

6. Optionally specify files that should be placed at the beginning of the disk during optimization. (See "To Place Files at the Beginning of a Disk.")

7. Optionally specify files that are not to be moved during optimization. (See "To Specify Unmovable Files.")

8. Optionally specify the method of optimization. (See "To Select an Optimization Method.")

9. Optionally set miscellaneous options. (See "To Set Miscellaneous SPEEDISK Options.")

10. Save the new configuration: Pull down the Configure menu, and select the **Save options to disk** option.

11. Pull down the Optimize menu and select the **Begin optimization** option, or press **Alt-B**. The optimization process may take some time to finish.

12. Select **OK** to acknowledge completion of the operation.

13. In the dialog box that appears, select **Another Drive** to defragment another drive, select **Configure** to change program configuration, or select **Exit to DOS** if you are finished. If you select Another Drive, go back to step 2. If you select Configure, go back to step 4.

## To Place Files at the Beginning of a Disk

1. Pull down the Configure menu, and select the **files to Place first** option.

2. In the Files to Place First dialog box, optionally add a filespec to the file list. Select **Insert** and type a filespec. Repeat as necessary.

3. Optionally remove a filespec from the file list by highlighting the filespec and selecting **Delete**. Repeat as necessary.

4. Optionally rearrange the order of the files. Highlight a filespec you want to relocate, select **Move** to tag the

filespec, use ↑ and ↓ or the mouse to relocate it, and select **Move** again to untag it. Repeat as necessary.

5. Select **OK**.

As a general rule, you get an increase in hard-disk performance if frequently accessed files (those that will not change in size, such as .COM or .EXE files) are placed at the beginning of the disk, thus minimizing the distance the read-write heads must go to find them. This function allows you to specify the files to be placed at the beginning of the disk.

## To Quit SPEEDISK

• Select the Quit! menu, or press **Esc**.

## To Save the Current Configuration

• Pull down the Configure menu, and select the **Save options to disk** option.

Saved settings remain in effect in the current session and in future sessions until they are changed again.

## To Select a Different Drive to Defragment/Optimize

1. Pull down the Optimize menu, and select the **Drive** option.

2. In the dialog box that appears, select the drive to defragment or optimize.

3. Go to step 3 in "To Defragment/Optimize a Hard Disk."

Use this function if, during configuration (steps 4–10), you want to defragment or optimize a different drive from the one you initially chose.

## To Select an Optimization Method

1. Pull down the Optimize menu, and select the **Optimization Method** option.

2. In the Select Optimization Method dialog box, select from five available options: **Full Optimization, Unfragment Files Only, Unfragment Free Space, Directory Optimization**, and **File Sort**.

3. Select **OK**.

In step 2, select Full Optimization to defragment all files and move all files and directories toward the front of the disk. If you select Unfragment Files Only, each file's clusters will be placed consecutively on the disk but files won't be moved toward the beginning of the disk. This option is faster than Full Optimization but not as thorough, because it can leave empty space between files.

Select Unfragment Free Space to move data forward to the beginning of the disk. This option does not defragment files but only fills empty space. Though faster than both of the previous options, it is not as effective. Select Directory Optimization to move only directories toward the front of the disk. Select File Sort to sort your files as they are listed in their directories. This is the function of the DS (Directory Sort) program in version 4.5. To specify the order in which files are listed, see "To Specify File Sort Order."

## To Set Miscellaneous SPEEDISK Options

1. Pull down the Configure menu, and select **Other options**.

2. Toggle any of three available options: **Read-after-Write, Use DOS Verify**, and **Clear unused space**.

3. Select **OK**.

In step 2, select Read-after-Write to check that data was properly written to a new location on disk. Select Use DOS Verify for the same reason you would use Read-after-Write. Use DOS Verify, however, is faster and less accurate. Select Clear Unused Space to have SPEEDISK wipe all unused space as data is relocated.

## To Specify Directory Order

1. Pull down the Configure menu, and select the **Directory order** option.

2. In the Select Directory Order dialog box, optionally high-light a directory in the Directory list box and select **Add** to add it to the Directory Order box. Repeat as necessary.

3. Optionally highlight a directory in the Directory Order box, and select **Delete** to remove it. Repeat as necessary.

4. Optionally rearrange files in the Directory Order box. Highlight the directory you want to relocate, select **Move** to tag it, use ↑ and ↓ or the mouse to reposition the direc-tory, and select **Move** again to untag it. Repeat as necessary.

5. Select **OK**.

Use this function to specify the order in which directories are writ-ten on the disk during Full Optimization or Directory Optimiza-tion. (See "To Select an Optimization Method.") As a general rule, the best performance results from placing the most frequently ac-cessed directories first. Directories are placed as they are listed in the Directory Order box in the Select Directory Order dialog box.

In step 2, you can move the highlight quickly by using built-in Speed Search. To use Speed Search, simply type the first letter or letters of the directory you want to highlight. Each time you type a letter, the highlight bar jumps to the next directory name beginning with the letter typed. Pressing Ctrl-⤶ cycles the highlight bar through all directories that match the current search string.

In step 4, some rearranging is usually necessary, because directories added to the Directory Order box are placed at the top of the list.

## To Specify File Sort Order

1. Pull down the Configure menu, and select the **File sort** op-tion. The File Sort dialog box appears.

2. In the Sort Criterion box, select how files are to be sorted.

3. In the Sort Order box, specify whether files are to be sorted in Ascending or Descending order.

4. Select **OK**.

Use this function to specify the order in which files will be listed in their directories. This sorting can be accomplished by a file sort or by any kind of optimization. (See "To Select an Optimization Method.")

In step 2, there are five options from which to choose:

- **Name**, to sort files by file name
- **Extension**, to sort files by file extension
- **Date & Time**, to sort files by file date and time
- **Size**, to sort files in order of their size
- **Unsorted**, to leave files in whatever order they may be in

In step 3, the Ascending and Descending options have no effect if the sort order is set to Unsorted in step 2.

## To Specify Unmovable Files

1. Pull down the Configure menu, and select the **Unmovable files** option.
2. In the Unmovable Files dialog box, type the complete name of a file that is not to be moved and press ↓. Repeat as necessary.
3. Optionally remove files from the list by highlighting them and selecting **Delete**.
4. Select **OK** when finished.

Some files, such as those employed by certain copy-protection schemes, should not be repositioned on the disk. SPEEDISK is good at identifying such files. This function allows for manual editing of the unmovable file list.

## To View a File Fragmentation Report

1. Pull down the Information menu, and select the **Fragmentation Report** option.
2. In the directory tree in the File Fragmentation Report dialog box, highlight a directory whose files you want to detail. Repeat as necessary.
3. Select **OK** when finished.

In step 2, you can move the highlight quickly by using built-in Speed Search. To use Speed Search, simply type the first letter or letters of the directory you want to highlight. Each time you type a letter, the highlight bar jumps to the next directory name beginning with the letter typed. Pressing Ctrl-⏎ cycles the highlight bar through all directories that match the current search string.

The report details the name of each file in the highlighted directory, the percentage of the file that is unfragmented, the total number of fragments that make up the file, and the number of clusters the file occupies.

Files that are moderately fragmented are shown in yellow on a color display and are bulleted on a monochrome display. Files that are highly fragmented are shown in red on a color display and are bulleted on a monochrome display. Files that are 100 percent unfragmented are displayed normally.

## To View the Map Legend

1. Pull down the Information menu, and select the Map **Legend** option.
2. Select **OK** when you are finished reading.

A partial legend appears on the screen with the disk map. Use this option to display a complete legend.

## To View Relevant Disk Information

1. Pull down the Information menu, and select the Disk **statistics** option.
2. Select **OK** when you are finished reading.

This function provides such information as disk size, percentage of disk space that is occupied and free, number of files on the disk, number of clusters allocated to files and directories, and number of unused clusters.

## To View a Static File List

1. Pull down the Information menu, and select the **Show static files** option.
2. Select **OK** when finished.

This function lists files deemed unmovable by SPEEDISK, as well as those specified as unmovable by the user. (See "To Specify Unmovable Files.")

## To Walk the Disk Map

1. Pull down the Information menu, and select the **Walk map** option.
2. Move the flashing block to the cluster whose contents you want to detail.
3. Select **OK** when you're finished reading the Contents of Map Block dialog box.
4. Repeat steps 2 and 3 as necessary.

This function details the contents of cluster blocks as they appear on the SPEEDISK disk map. Specifically, it shows which clusters are represented by the block, which files belong to the clusters, and whether the clusters are optimized or fragmented.

In step 2, you can move the flashing block with the mouse or the cursor keys. When using the mouse, drag the flashing block or simply click on the target cluster. When using the arrow keys, press ↵ to detail the target cluster.

After step 3, you can detail other blocks. When finished, if you have been using the arrow keys and the flashing block is still visible, press the Escape key. If you have been using the mouse, simply select the next function you want to perform.

## ● SYNTAX

**SPEEDISK (*drive*:) ( */options*)**

**drive:** specifies the drive to defragment/optimize. If you specify *drive:* on the command line, omit step 2 in "To Defragment/ Optimize a Hard Disk."

The options are the following:

**/B** reboots the computer after defragmentation/optimization.

**/C** specifies a full disk optimization. (See "To Select an Optimization Method.")

**/D** specifies a directory optimization. (See "To Select an Optimization Method.")

**/Q** specifies Unfragment Free Space. (See "To Select an Optimization Method.")

**/SD(-)** sorts files by date and time. Append the optional hyphen to sort in descending order.

**/SE(-)** sorts files by extension. Append the optional hyphen to sort in descending order.

**/SN(-)** sorts files by file name. Append the optional hyphen to sort in descending order.

**/SS(-)** sorts files by file size. Append the optional hyphen to sort in descending order.

**/U** specifies Unfragment Files Only. (See "To Select an Optimization Method.")

**/V** toggles the Read-after-Write option on. (See "To Set Miscellaneous SPEEDISK Options.")

# SYSINFO
## *System Information*

SYSINFO provides 17 screens of information about most aspects of your computer. It details system configuration, gives complete characteristics of installed drives, details memory usage, and provides CPU and hard-disk benchmarks.

● **UPGRADE INFORMATION**  SYSINFO is a considerably expanded descendant of the SI (System Information) program in version 4.5. The information provided by DI (Disk Information) in 4.5 can also be found in SYSINFO.

## To Cycle through Information Screens Consecutively

*   At the bottom of any information screen, select **Next** to see the next screen in sequence. Select **Previous** to see the previous one.

The order in which information screens appear corresponds to the order of options on the pull-down menus. The first screen (System Summary) is the first option on the first menu, the second screen is the second option, and so on.

## To Print a Complete System Summary Report

1.  Pull down the Report menu, and select P**rint report.**
2.  In the Report Options dialog box, select the information screens you want to include in the report.
3.  In the User Text box, optionally toggle the **Report header** option to include a header in the report.
4.  Optionally toggle the **Notes at end of report** option to append comments at the end of the report.
5.  Select **Printer** to send the report to your printer. Select **File** to send the report to a file.

6. If you are printing to a file, type the path and file name to which you want output sent, and select **OK**.

7. If you are printing to a file, select **OK** to acknowledge completion.

This function allows you to print the contents of multiple information screens in one report. The Report Options dialog box has an option for every information screen in SYSINFO.

Toggling the Report Header option on in step 3 adds an additional step to the sequence between steps 6 and 7: In the Report Header dialog box, type your header and select **OK**.

Toggling the Notes at End of Report option on in step 4 also adds an additional step between steps 6 and 7: In the User Notes dialog box, type your comments and select **OK**. Comments can occupy a maximum of ten lines. Move the cursor between lines by using ↑ and ↓ only. Pressing ↵ terminates input and is equivalent to selecting OK.

## To Print an Information Screen

1. Select the **Print** option at the bottom of the information screen.

2. In the Print Current Information dialog box, select **Printer** to send the output to your printer. Select **File** to send output to a file.

3. If you are printing to a file, type the path and file name to which you want output sent, and select **OK**.

4. Select **OK** to acknowledge completion.

Omit step 3 if you are printing to the printer and not to a file.

## To Quit SYSINFO

• Select the Quit! menu, or press **Esc**.

## To View a Particular Information Screen

Each information screen can be accessed by selecting one option on one menu. (See Table 2 for details.) The screens show the following information:

- *System Configuration:* type of main processor, math coprocessor, BIOS, video standard, mouse, keyboard, bus, amount of memory installed, number and types of drives, number of ports, and type of operating system running.

- *Video Card:* kind of card installed, kind of monitor installed, current video mode, character size, maximum number of on-screen scan lines, amount of video memory, video page size, and address of first segment of video memory.

- *Hardware Interrupts:* hardware interrupt usage.

- *Software Interrupts:* software interrupt usage.

- *Network:* current user and type of network (SYSINFO is only compatible with Novell Netware networks).

- *CMOS:* status and contents of CMOS, including type and number of installed drives and amount and kind of memory installed.

- *Installed Drives:* number of drives installed, drive letters assigned to them, and their type, capacity, and current default directory.

- *Specific Drive:* logical and physical characteristics of any drive on your system (select the drive in the drive list box in the upper-right corner of the Disk Characteristics screen).

- *Partition Table:* location and contents of partition table.

- *System Memory:* kind and amount of memory installed, how much is used, and how much is free.

- *Installed TSRs:* name, location in memory, and size of TSRs loaded.

- *640K of DOS Memory:* details on first 640K of memory, listing what applications are loaded, the starting address and size of each application, and to what each belongs.

- *Installed Device Drivers:* devices loaded, the starting memory address, and description of each.

**Table 2:** Information Screens in SYSINFO

| SCREEN | MENU | OPTION |
|---|---|---|
| System Configuration | System | System summary |
| Video Card | System | Video summary |
| Hardware Interrupts | System | Hardware interrupts |
| Software Interrupts | System | Software interrupts |
| Network | System | Network information |
| CMOS | System | CMOS status |
| Installed Drives | Disks | Disk summary |
| Specific Drive | Disks | disk Characteristics |
| Partition Table | Disks | Partition Tables |
| System Memory | Memory | memory Usage summary |
| Installed TSRs | Memory | TSR programs |
| 640K of DOS Memory | Memory | memory Block list |
| Installed Device Drivers | Memory | Device drivers |
| CPU Speed | Benchmarks | CPU speed |
| Hard-Disk Speed | Benchmarks | Hard disk speed |
| Overall System Speed | Benchmarks | Overall Performance Index |
| Network Speed | Benchmarks | Network Performance Speed |
| AUTOEXEC.BAT File | Report | view AUTOEXEC.BAT |
| CONFIG.SYS File | Report | view CONFIG.SYS |

- *CPU Speed:* speed of CPU relative to Compaq 386/33, IBM PC/AT (8 MHz), and IBM PC/XT (4.77 MHz).

- *Hard-Disk Speed:* speed of hard disk relative to hard disks that come standard with Compaq 386/33, IBM PC/AT (8 MHz), and IBM PC/XT (4.77 MHz); average access times commonly used for comparing hard disks.

- *Overall System Speed:* combination of CPU speed and hard-disk speed tests, comparing overall speed with Compaq 386/33, IBM PC/AT (8 MHz), and IBM PC/XT (4.77 MHz).

- *Network Speed:* read and write tests of network server's hard disk, measuring throughput in kilobytes per second.

- *AUTOEXEC.BAT File:* display of AUTOEXEC.BAT file.

- *CONFIG.SYS File:* display of CONFIG.SYS file.

## ● SYNTAX

### SYSINFO ( */options*)

The options are the following:

**/AUTO:**# cycles continuously through all information screens at intervals of # seconds. Press the Escape key to stop and return to DOS.

**/DEMO** cycles continuously through the System Summary screen and Benchmark screens at 5-second intervals. Press the Escape key to stop and return to DOS.

**/N** starts SYSINFO without memory scan.

**/SOUND** sounds a beep after each test of the CPU when you run the Benchmarks CPU Speed option.

**/SUMMARY** displays the System Summary screen without loading the SYSINFO program shell. This is identical to the SI (System Information) program in version 4.5.

**/TSR** displays a list of loaded TSRs.

# UNERASE

UNERASE enables you to recover all or parts of erased files. When a file is erased, its entry is removed from the directory structure and the FAT (file allocation table). The file's data, however, remains on the disk, making unerasure possible. If an erased file's data is not overwritten by another file that uses the same disk space, UNERASE can recover the erased file in its entirety. If erased data is partially overwritten, UNERASE allows you to reassemble the remaining parts manually.

● **UPGRADE INFORMATION**  UNERASE contains the file recovery functions of the NU (Norton Utilities) and QU (Quick Unerase) programs in version 4.5. It can recover a deleted directory, as UD (Unremove Directory) in 4.5 did, and can also search for text on the erased portions of a disk, as TS (Text Search) in 4.5 did.

## To Add Data to an Existing File

1. Highlight the file to which you want to add data.
2. Pull down the File menu, and select the **aPpend to** option.
3. Go to step 4 in "To Unerase a File Manually."

This function allows you to add clusters manually to a file that already exists or has been unerased. It is only available if you highlight an existing file. Therefore, you may have to toggle the **Include non-erased files** option on. To find out how to do this, see "To Include Existing Files on the File List."

## To Change the Current Directory

1. Pull down the File menu and select the **change diRectory** option, or press **Alt-R**.
2. In the Change Directory dialog box, highlight the directory to which you want to change, and select **OK**.

In step 2, you can move the highlight quickly by using built-in Speed Search. To use Speed Search, simply type the first letter or letters of the directory you want to highlight. Each time you type a letter, the highlight bar jumps to the next directory name beginning with the letter typed. Pressing Ctrl-↵ cycles the highlight bar through all directories that match the current search string.

Because directories always appear on the file list, some directory navigation is also possible from the file list itself. Double-clicking or pressing ↵ when a directory is highlighted makes that directory the current one.

## To Change the Current Drive

1. Pull down the File menu and select the **change** D**rive** option, or press **Alt-D**.

2. In the Change Drive dialog box, select a drive.

## To Include Existing Files on the File List

- Pull down the Options menu, and select the **Include non-erased files** option.

This option is a toggle. When toggled on, both erased and existing files appear on the file list. When toggled off, only erased files appear. This option is not available when the file list displays the results of a search (see "To Search for Erased Files in Erased Directories," "To Search Erased Disk Space for Specific Text," and "To Search for Deleted Data Fragments").

## To List All Files on the Current Drive

- Pull down the File menu and select the **view** All **directories** option, or press **Alt-A**.

Use this function to display all files on the current drive. You can list all files or only erased files (see "To Include Existing Files on the File List").

## To List Files in the Current Directory Only

- Pull down the File menu and select the **view Current directory** option, or press **Alt-C**.

Use this function to display only the current directory on the file list. You can list all files or only erased files (see "To Include Existing Files on the File List").

## To Quit UNERASE

- Select the Quit! menu, or press **Esc**.

## To Rename a File

1. Highlight the file you want to rename.
2. Pull down the File menu, and select the **reName** option.
3. In the Rename dialog box, type the new file name and select **OK**.

This function is only available if the highlighted file already exists or has been recovered. (See "To Include Existing Files on the File List" if you want existing files on the file list.) It is not available if any files have been tagged.

## To Resume a Discontinued Search

- Pull down the Search menu, and select the **Continue search** option.

Use this function to resume a search (for lost names, text, or data types) that you have interrupted.

## To Search for Deleted Data Fragments

1. Pull down the Search menu, and select the **for Data types** option.
2. In the Search for Data Types dialog box, select the data types for which you want to search.
3. Select **OK**.

This function searches the erased portion of the disk for specific kinds of data. In step 2, select one of the following options:

- **Normal Text**, to search for ASCII text
- **Lotus 1-2-3 and Symphony**, to search for Lotus and compatible spreadsheet data
- **dBASE**, to search for database data
- **Other data**, to search for anything else

When a match is found, the cluster or clusters containing the search string are given a file name and appear on the file list, available for unerasure (see "To Unerase a File or Group of Files Automatically"). File names begin with FILE0000; subsequent file names are numbered sequentially. The appended extensions depend on the kind of data contained in the file. Text files have the .TXT extension, database files have .DBF, spreadsheet files have .WK1, and all others have .DAT.

## To Search Erased Disk Space for Specific Text

1. Pull down the Search menu, and select the **for Text** option.
2. In the Search for Text dialog box, type the string for which you want to search.
3. Optionally toggle the **Ignore case** option off for a case-sensitive search.
4. Select **OK**.

This function searches erased disk space for text you specify. When a match is found, the cluster or clusters containing the search string are given a file name and appear on the file list, available for unerasure (see "To Unerase a File or Group of Files Automatically"). File names begin with FILE0000; subsequent file names are numbered sequentially.

In step 3, the Ignore Case switch toggles case-sensitive searches on or off. If it is turned on (the default), then the search is not case-sensitive. Searching for *Linda* will find every consecutive occurrence of the letters *l-i–n-d-a* without regard to case: *Linda, LINDA, LiNdA*, etc. If it is turned off, then the search will only find exact matches of the search string. Searching for *Linda* will only find *Linda*, and not *LINDA, linda, lInDa*, etc.

## To Search for Erased Files in Erased Directories

- Pull down the Search menu, and select the **for Lost names** option.

The names of erased files are kept in existing directories and are listed for unerasure on the file list. When a directory is deleted, however, the names of deleted files contained in the directory cannot be so easily accessed. This function searches the disk for the names of erased files in erased directories—lost names. When found, the lost files can be unerased, completely or partially, depending on how much of their data has been overwritten (see "To Unerase a File or Group of Files Automatically" and "To Unerase a File Manually").

## To Sort the File List

1. Pull down the Options menu.
2. Select one of the six available sort options.

In step 2, select one of the following options:

- **sort by Name**, to sort the file list by name
- **sort by Extension**, to sort by file extension
- **sort by Time**, to sort by file date and time—only available when viewing files in the current directory (see "To List Files in the Current Directory Only")
- **sort by Size**, to sort by file size
- **sort by Directory**, to sort alphabetically by directory— available when viewing all files on the current drive (see "To List All Files on the Current Drive")
- **sort by Prognosis**, to sort by prognosis for successful recovery

## To Specify the Range of a Search

1. Pull down the Search menu, and select the **set search Range** option.

2.  In the Search Range dialog box and at the **Starting Cluster:** prompt, type the number of the first cluster of the range you want to search.

3.  At the **Ending Cluster:** prompt, type the number of the last cluster in the range you want to search.

4.  Select **OK**.

When you start a search, UNERASE, by default, searches the entire current disk. Use this function if you want to limit searches to particular parts of the current disk.

## To Tag a File for Unerasure

1.  Highlight the file you want to tag.

2.  Pull down the File menu and select the S**elect** option, or press the spacebar, or click the right mouse button.

Select option is only available when an untagged file is highlighted.

## To Tag a Group of Files for Unerasure

1.  Pull down the File menu and select the **select** Group option or press the gray plus key on the numeric keypad.

2.  In the Select dialog box, type a filespec for the files you want to tag (*.TXT, *.DOC, *.*, etc.), and select **OK**.

## To Unerase a File or Group of Files Automatically

1.  Highlight or tag the file(s) you want to unerase.

2.  Select **Unerase** on the file list.

3.  In the Unerase dialog box, optionally toggle the **Prompt for missing 1st letters** option off and select **Unerase**.

4.  Enter the first letter of the file name.

UNERASE makes the automatic unerasure of files simple and straightforward. It is merely a matter of manipulating the file list to show the file you want to unerase.

In step 1, see "To Tag a File for Unerasure" and "To Tag a Group of Files for Unerasure" if necessary.

In step 3, an erased file loses the first letter of its file name. When unerasing a file, therefore, the first letter of the file name must be supplied. Toggle the Prompt for Missing 1st Letters option off if you do not want to supply the first letter for each file. This causes UNERASE to make *a* the first letter of each unerased file. Omit step 3 if you are unerasing only one highlighted file, that is, if you have not actually tagged any files.

Omit step 4 if the Prompt for Missing 1st Letters option is toggled off in step 3.

## To Unerase a File Manually

1.  Highlight the file you want to unerase.
2.  Pull down the File menu and select the **Manual unerase** option, or press **Alt-M**.
3.  In the Unerase dialog box, enter the first letter of the erased file's name.
4.  In the Manual Unerase dialog box, select **Add cluster**.
5.  In the Add Clusters dialog box, select one of the four options for adding a cluster or group of clusters to the file.
6.  Optionally select **view File** to see the contents of the clusters assembled so far. Select **OK** in the View File dialog box when you're finished.
7.  Optionally select **view Map** to see the area(s) on the disk map used by the assembled clusters. Select **OK** in the View Map dialog box when you're finished.
8.  Repeat steps 4–7 as necessary.
9.  Select **Save** to save the unerased file.

Unerasing a file manually requires that you assemble (steps 4 and 5) and save (step 9) a file's component clusters. So that you can keep track, all assembled clusters are listed by number in the Added Clusters box in the Manual Unerase dialog box. You can unerase only one file at a time, even if more than one file on the file list is tagged.

In step 5, select one of the following options:

- **All clusters**, to have UNERASE assemble all the clusters likely to belong to the file
- **Next probable**, to have UNERASE add only the next most probable cluster
- **Data search**, to add clusters by searching for specific data
- **Cluster number**, to assemble a specific cluster or range of clusters

If you select Data Search, follow these steps before going to step 6:

- In the Data Search dialog box, enter a search string in ASCII characters at the **ASCII** prompt or in hex characters at the **Hex** prompt.
- Optionally toggle the **Ignore case** option off for a case-sensitive search.
- Select **Find**.
- When a match is found, it appears in the View File dialog box. Select **Hex** to view the data as hex characters or **Text** to view the data as ASCII characters.
- Select **Add cluster** if you want to add the cluster containing the match to the list of assembled clusters.
- Select **Find next** to search for the next occurrence of the search string.
- Repeat the fourth, fifth, and sixth steps if necessary.
- Select **Done** when you are finished searching and have gathered the clusters you want to add to the file.

If you select Cluster Number, follow these steps before going to step 6:

- In the Cluster Number dialog box and at the **Starting Cluster:** prompt, type the number of the first cluster in the range of clusters you want to add to the file.
- At the **Ending Cluster:** prompt, type the name of the last cluster in the range of clusters.
- Select **OK**.

In step 9, the clusters you have assembled or added will be recovered as one file. If, however, the clusters you have assembled are, taken together, smaller than the original file, there is one extra step: In the Confirm Save dialog box, select **Save anyway** to save what you have, or select **Resume** to go back to step 4.

## To Unerase a File to a New File Name Manually

1.  Highlight the file you want to unerase.
2.  Pull down the File menu, and select the **create File** option.
3.  In the UnErase dialog box, type the new file name and select **OK**.
4.  Go to step 4 in "To Unerase a File Manually."

This function allows you to erase a file manually and to give the file a name different from its original name.

## To Unerase a File to a New Location Automatically

1.  Highlight the file you want to unerase.
2.  Pull down the File menu, and select the **unerase To** option.
3.  In the Unerase To dialog box, select a new drive for the unerased file.
4.  Edit the suggested path and file name as needed, and select **OK**.

In step 4, you have to edit the suggested path if you want to place the unerased file in a subdirectory of the drive you specified in step 3, or if you want to supply the correct first letter of the file name. Erased files lose the first letter of the file name, so UNERASE automatically attaches an *a* during this procedure.

## To Untag a Group of Files

1.  Pull down the File menu and select the **Unselect group** option or press the gray minus key on the numeric keypad.

2.  In the Unselect dialog box, type the filespec for the files
    you want to untag (*.DOC, *.*, etc.), and select **OK**.

The Unselect Group option is only available when one or more files
are tagged.

## To Untag a Single File

1.  Highlight the tagged file you want to untag.
2.  Pull down the File menu and select the **unSelect** option,
    or press the spacebar, or click the right mouse button.

Unselect option is only available when a tagged file is highlighted.

## To View the Contents of a File on the File List

1.  Highlight the file whose contents you want to view.
2.  Select the **View** option at the bottom of the file list.
3.  In the View File dialog box, select **OK** when finished.

In step 3, the View File dialog box has other options. If the file is
presented in text mode, select **Hex** to view the file in hex characters.
If the file is presented in hex mode, select **Text** to view the file in
ASCII characters. Select **Next** to view the next file on the file list,
and select **Prev** to view the previous file on the file list.

## To View Pertinent
## Information about a File on the File List

1.  Highlight the file about which you want information.
2.  Select the **Info** option at the bottom of the file list.
3.  In the Information dialog box, select **OK** when finished.

This function shows the erased file's name, date, time, size, attributes, prognosis for unerasure, the number of its starting cluster,
and the number of clusters that comprise the file.

In step 3, the Information dialog box has two other options. Select **Next** to view information about the next file on the file list. Select **Prev** to view information about the previous file.

## ● SYNTAX

**UNERASE (*filespec*)**

**filespec** specifies the name of the file or group of files you want to unerase. If *filespec* is just a file name, *filespec* is unerased automatically, and the program returns you to the DOS prompt. (This function resembles QU (Quick Unerase) in version 4.5.) If, however, *filespec* uses wildcards, the unerase program comes up with all files matching *filespec* tagged. You must then take appropriate steps to unerase these files. (See "To Unerase a File or Group of Files Automatically" and "To Unerase a File Manually.")

# UNFORMAT

UNFORMAT recovers data on disks that have been formatted accidentally. UNFORMAT works best when critical system information (the boot record, root directory, and file allocation table, or FAT) has been saved with IMAGE or SFORMAT (Safe Format). Data can also be recovered when critical system information is not saved, though files will be placed in generically named directories (DIR0, DIR1, etc.). UNFORMAT will not work on disks that are completely overwritten when formatted (as floppy disks are when formatted with the FORMAT command in DOS). UNFORMAT can also be used to reconstruct some severely damaged disks.

● **UPGRADE INFORMATION**    UNFORMAT is a direct descendant of the FR (Format Recover) program in version 4.5. FR's ability to save critical system information, however, is contained in the IMAGE program.

## To Unformat a Disk

1. In the Unformat dialog box, select **Continue**.
2. In the dialog box that appears, select the drive you want to unformat.
3. When asked whether you saved IMAGE (critical system) information on the drive to be unformatted, select the appropriate response, **Yes** or **No**.
4. Select **Yes** in the confirmation box that appears.
5. The next few step differs depending on your selection in step 3:

    ● If you selected **Yes** in step 3 and IMAGE information has been saved on the disk to be unformatted, then select **OK** in the Image Info Found dialog box to unformat the disk using IMAGE information, select **Yes** in the Absolutely Sure confirmation box, and select **Full** in the Full or Partial Restore dialog box.

- If you selected **Yes** in step 3 and IMAGE information has not been saved, select **Yes** in the dialog box to unformat the disk without the IMAGE information.
- If you selected **No** in step 3, go to step 6.

**6.** Select **OK**, twice if necessary, to acknowledge completion of unformatting.

In the Full or Partial Restore dialog box, you can select **Partial** to restore all or only some of the disk's critical system information. Toggle any of the system areas you want to restore: **Boot Record**, **File Allocation Table**, or **Root Directory**. Then select **OK**.

In step 6, selecting OK a second time is necessary when a disk without IMAGE information is unformatted. The second OK acknowledges the generic directories (DIR0, DIR1) into which recovered files are placed.

## ● SYNTAX

### UNFORMAT (*drive:*)

**drive:** specifies the drive to be unformatted. If you specify a drive on the command line, you can skip steps 1 and 2 in "To Unformat a Disk."

**See Also**   IMAGE, SFORMAT

# WIPEINFO
## *The Secure Deletion Program*

WIPEINFO allows you to dispose of private data securely. When you delete a file from a disk, it is removed from the directory and the file allocation table (FAT), but its data remain on the disk, making it possible to unerase the file. When you use WIPEINFO, however, the data are completely overwritten, making recovery impossible. WIPEINFO can expunge entire disks or files that you specify.

● **UPGRADE INFORMATION**   WIPEINFO combines the features of WIPEFILE and WIPEDISK in version 4.5.

## To Configure WIPEINFO

1. In the WipeInfo dialog box, select **Configure**.
2. In the Wipe Configuration dialog box, select a wipe method (see Figure 7).
3. Select a concomitant wipe value.

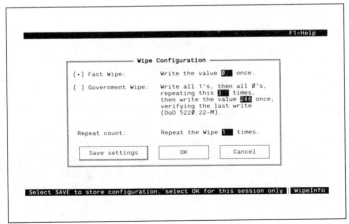

**Figure 7:** The Wipe Configuration dialog box

4. At the **Repeat count**: prompt, enter the number of times you want to repeat the wipe.

5. Select **OK** to set these options for the current WIPEINFO session only, or select **Save Settings** to set options for both current and future sessions.

In step 2, there are two wipe methods available: Select **Fast Wipe:** simply to overwrite data (this is sufficient protection against all but the most sophisticated electronic snoops), or select **Government Wipe:** if you work for the Department of Defense or have a security clearance.

In step 3, select the character that WIPEINFO uses to overwrite data by typing its numeric value. For a Fast Wipe, the default is 0. For a Government wipe, you also select the number of times WIPEINFO overwrites with 1's and 0's before it writes with the character you specify. The defaults for this option are 3 and ASCII character 246, respectively.

## To Overwrite the Contents of an Entire Disk

1. In the WipeInfo dialog box, select **Drives**. The Wipe Drives dialog box appears.

2. In the Drives box, select the drive or drives to be overwritten.

3. In the Wiping Method box, select the areas of the disk(s) to be overwritten.

4. Select **Wipe**.

5. In the Warning dialog box, select **Wipe**.

6. Select **OK** to acknowledge completion.

In step 2, every drive installed on your system appears in the Drives box. Toggle the drive or drives you want to delete.

In step 3, select **Wipe entire drive** if you want to overwrite all of a disk. Select **Wipe unused areas only** to overwrite disk space not containing data. This option allows you to preserve data currently on a disk while destroying data from earlier erasures using the DEL command in DOS.

## To Wipe Files from a Disk

1.  In the WipeInfo dialog box, select **Files**. The Wipe Files dialog box appears.

2.  In the File Name box, enter a filespec indicating the file or groups of files to be wiped. Preface the filespec with a new path if necessary.

3.  Optionally toggle any or all of four file options: **Include subdirs**, **Confirm each file**, **Hidden files**, or **Read-Only files**.

4.  In the Wiping Method box, specify the areas to be wiped and the method to be used.

5.  Select **Wipe**.

6.  In the Warning dialog box, select **Wipe**. If **Confirm each file** is toggled on, select **Wipe**, **Skip**, or **Auto** in the Wiping Files dialog box.

7.  Select **OK** to acknowledge completion.

In step 2, the current directory is supplied as a path. To change this path, type a new one or select the **Directory** option at the bottom of the Wipe Files dialog box. In the Change Directory dialog box that appears, type a new default directory in the Current Directory box, or select a new directory in the Sub-directories and Drives boxes. You must enter a filespec (*.doc, *.*, file.ext, etc.) in addition to the path. Omitting the filespec causes an error.

In step 3, there are four options you can toggle:

*   **Hidden files**, to overwrite hidden files matching the filespec supplied in step 2. Hidden files will not be wiped unless this option is toggled on.

*   **Read-Only files**, to overwrite read-only files matching the filespec supplied in step 2. Read-only files will not be wiped unless this option is toggled on.

*   **Include subdirs**, to wipe files in subdirectories beneath the specified path.

*   **Confirm each file**, to selectively wipe out or keep each file matching the specified filespec.

In step 4, select one of three options:

- **Wipe files**, to overwrite the specified files.
- **Delete files only, don't wipe** to *delete*, not wipe, files. This is equivalent to using the DEL command in DOS; the file name is removed from the directory structure and the FAT, but the data remain on disk (thus, you can still recover the files by using Unerase).
- **Wipe unused file slack only**, to keep files intact on disk but to overwrite each file's slack area.

The *slack* is unused space assigned to a file. If, for example, the cluster size on a hard disk is 2K (2048 bytes) and a file called EXAMPLE is 3100 bytes large, the file occupies one entire cluster and part of a second. Both clusters, including the unused part of the second cluster—the slack—are assigned to EXAMPLE in the FAT. As files change size and are deleted, slack areas fill up with data.

If you toggle Confirm Each File on, select **Wipe** to overwrite a file, **Skip** to keep the file intact on disk, or **Auto** to wipe automatically all remaining files matching the supplied filespec.

## ● SYNTAX

**WIPEINFO (*drive:*) ( */options*)**

or

**WIPEINFO (*filespec*) ( */options*)**

**drive:** specifies the drive to be wiped.

**filespec** specifies the file or files to be wiped.

The options are the following:

**/E** overwrites unoccupied or erased disk space, leaving data intact. Use this option when you specify a drive, not a file.

**/G** uses Government Wipe.

**/K** overwrites file slack, leaving files intact. Use this option when you specify a file, not a drive.

**/N** deletes files; it works like the DEL command in DOS. Use this option when you specify a file, not a drive.

**/R#** repeats the wipe a specified number of times.

**/S** wipes files in all subdirectories below the default directory. Use this option when you specify a file, not a drive.

**/V#** overwrites data with the specified ASCII value.

# APPENDIX
## Installing the Norton Utilities

Installing the Norton Utilities is made easy by its installation program. The procedure is straightforward and is the same whether you are using 5¼- or 3½-inch disks. You must have 2.5 megabytes of free space in memory to do a complete installation.

## INSTALLING THE PROGRAM

To install the Norton Utilities 5.0, follow these steps:

1. Put the Installation Disk in drive A. Although you can install Norton from any floppy drive, drive A is used here for convenience.

2. Type **a:install** and press ↵. (If the Installation Disk is in a drive other than A, preface *install* with the appropriate drive letter.)

3. In the Norton Utilities 5.0 Install dialog box, select **Black & White** if you have a monochrome display or a laptop computer. Select **Color** if you have a color display.

4. If you see a Warning! dialog box, select **Continue**.

5. If you see an information screen, select **Continue** when you've finished reading.

6. Select **New Install** if you are installing the program for the first time. Select **Reconfigure** if you have already installed the program and want to change some of its settings. If you select Reconfigure, go to step 15.

7. Select **Full Install** to install the entire Norton Utilities package. Select **Partial Install** to install only selected programs. (If you select Partial Install, toggle only the programs you want to install and select **Continue**.)

8. In the Install dialog box, select the drive that you are using to install the Norton Utilities.

9. In the Norton Utilities 5.0 Install dialog box and in the **Put Utilities files in:** box, type the drive and path to which the Norton Utilities is to be copied.

10. Select **Continue** and then wait while files are unarchived and copied from the Installation Disk.

11. Place the disk you are prompted for in the drive indicated and select **Continue**. Then wait while files are unarchived and copied.

12. Repeat step 11 until you are no longer prompted to insert disks.

13. When you are finished inserting disks, you have the option to give five programs shorter, mnemonic names. Toggle the programs you want to rename and select **Continue**.

14. If you want to use Norton's SFORMAT as your default format program, select **Continue**. If not, select **Skip This**. Choosing this option changes the name of all programs named FORMAT.* to XXFORMAT.* and SFORMAT.EXE to FORMAT.EXE.

15. Optionally select **Password** to password-protect selected programs. If you select Password, follow these steps:

    • In the Set Password Protection dialog box, toggle the programs you want to password-protect and select **Continue**.

    • At the **Enter a password:** prompt, type a password and press ⏎.

    • At the **Verify your password:** prompt, retype your password and press ⏎.

16. Optionally select **Norton Program** to enable or disable editing of the program list in the NORTON program. If you select Norton Program, follow these steps:

    • Toggle **Disable Editing** to disallow changes to the NORTON program list. Toggle **Enable Editing** to allow changes.

    • Select **Continue**.

17. Optionally select **Hardware** to set video and mouse options. Selecting Hardware brings up the Video and Mouse Options dialog box, which is identical to the one available in the NORTON program. (See "To Configure the Norton

Utilities" in the NORTON section of this book for a complete explanation.) Toggle the options you want and
select **Save**.

18. Optionally select **System Files** to edit your
AUTOEXEC.BAT and CONFIG.SYS files. (See "To
Edit AUTOEXEC.BAT" and "To Edit CONFIG.SYS.")

19. Select **Done**.

20. If you have modified AUTOEXEC.BAT or CONFIG.SYS,
select **Reboot**. If you haven't modified these files, select
**Go to Utilities** to quit to the directory that contains the
Norton Utilities. Select **Return to DOS** to quit to the
default directory.

## To Edit AUTOEXEC.BAT

1. After selecting System Files in step 18 of the installation
procedure, select **AUTOEXEC.BAT**.

2. Select **Continue**.

3. Select **Add** to place the directory containing the Norton
Utilities in your system path automatically. This allows
you to run the Norton Utilities from anywhere, regardless
of the current directory. Select **Skip** if you do not want to
modify your path.

4. Select **Add** to add the NU environment variable to your
AUTOEXEC.BAT file automatically. This allows the program to find its configuration files if they are located outside the directory containing the Norton Utilities. Select
**Skip** if you don't want to add the environment variable.

5. Optionally toggle **Disk Monitor** and/or **File Save** if you
want to load these programs when you boot your computer, then select **Add**. Select **Skip** if you don't want these
programs loaded when you boot your computer.

6. Select **Add** if you want to save critical disk information
with the IMAGE program each time you boot your computer. This guards against accidental formatting of your
hard disk. (See also the IMAGE and UNFORMAT sections
in this book.) Select **Skip** if you don't want to save disk
information.

7. Select **Add** if you want to run a quick surface test of your hard disk (NDD /QUICK) each time you boot your computer. Select **Skip** if you don't.

8. If you have made any changes to your AUTOEXEC.BAT file, you have the chance to review them.

   • If you want to reorder any of the changes, highlight the amended line you want to move. Select **Move** to tag it (clicking the right mouse button or pressing the spacebar has the same effect). Use ↑ and ↓ or click the left mouse button to relocate it. Select **Move** again to untag the line in its new position. Repeat this as necessary.

   • Select **Save** to accept the changes you've made.

   • Select **Discard** to cancel *all* changes made to AUTOEXEC.BAT and to leave the file as it was before installation.

## To Edit CONFIG.SYS

1. After selecting System Files in step 18 of the installation procedure, select **CONFIG.SYS**.

2. Select **Continue**.

3. If you want to load one of the Norton CACHE programs, toggle **Fast Cache** or **Small Cache** and select **Add**. Select **Skip** if you don't.

4. Select **Add** if you want to enable the use of encrypted drives from the DISKREET program. Select **Skip** if you don't. (This step is omitted if you haven't installed DISKREET.)

5. If you have made any changes to your CONFIG.SYS file, you have the chance to review them.

   • If you want to reorder any of the changes, highlight the amended line you want to move. Select **Move** to tag it (clicking the right mouse button or pressing the spacebar has the same effect). Use ↑ and ↓ or click the left mouse button to relocate it. Select **Move** again to untag the line in its new position. Repeat this as necessary.

- Select **Save** to accept the changes you've made.
- Select **Discard** to cancel *all* changes made to CONFIG.SYS and to leave the file as it was before installation.

# MODIFYING YOUR CONFIG.SYS FILE MANUALLY

Modifying the CONFIG.SYS file is the means by which device drivers are loaded. Device drivers are necessary to run certain peripherals and programs. If you do not want to modify your CONFIG.SYS file during installation, you can always go back and do it later. With the Norton Utilities, this is necessary if you want to use encrypted drives through the DISKREET program, if you want to load one of the CACHE programs from CONFIG.SYS and not AUTOEXEC.BAT, or if you want to use the color options in some of the BE functions.

To use encrypted drives, the DISKREET.SYS driver must be loaded. To load this driver, the following line must appear in your CON-FIG.SYS file:

**device=*drive:*\*path*\DISKREET.SYS**

where *drive*: is the drive on which DISKREET.SYS is located and *path* is the subdirectory in which DISKREET.SYS resides.

To load a cache from CONFIG.SYS, the following line must appear:

**device=*drive:*\*path*\NCACHE-(F¦S).EXE**

where *drive*: is the drive on which NCACHE-F or NCACHE-S is located and *path* is the subdirectory in which NCACHE-F or NCACHE-S resides.

To use colored windows, boxes, etc., with BE, the ANSI.SYS driver must be loaded. The following line must appear:

**device=*drive:*\*path* \ANSI.SYS**

where *drive*: is the drive on which ANSI.SYS is located and *path* is the subdirectory in which ANSI.SYS resides.

The CONFIG.SYS file must be in ASCII format. To modify it, you can use any word processor that allows you to save a file in pure ASCII format.

# 158

# Index

active windows, switching, 28
Advise menu
    CHKDSK error messages, 109–110
    Common Disk Problems option, 108–109
    DOS error messages, 110
Alt key, for pull-down menus, x
ANSI.SYS driver, 5, 88
archive files, 34
ASCII characters, 32
    in hex view, 13–14
ASK command (BE), 1–2
ASSIGN command (DOS), 10
Auto View option, 28, 31
auto-close timeouts, 50–51
AUTOEXEC.BAT file, 130, 155–156
Average Seek, 8

background color, 5, 88
Backspace key, xii
BACKUP command (DOS), 34
backup programs, archive attribute and, 34
bad clusters, 16, 59
<BAD> marker, 16
base conversions, 32
batch files, 4, 63–64
BE (Batch Enhancer), 1–6
    help from, xiii
BEEP command (BE), 2–3
Bernoulli boxes, 10
BIOS Seek Overhead, 7–8
blanking out screen display, 49
block of data
    copying, 11–12
    moving, 23–24
boot record
    editing, 11–12
    linking to, 23
    protecting, 38
    saving, 81
bootable disks, 34, 56, 114
border color, 5
BOX command (BE), 3
branching, 2, 4

caches, 9, 83, 156–157
CALIBRAT, 7–10
Character Filters setting, 31
CHKDSK error messages, 109–110
clearing screen display, 3–4

clipboard, 11–13
Clipper files, 71
CLS command (BE), 3–4
cluster chains, linking to, 23
clusters, 8, 117
    adding, 133
    bad, 16, 59
    editing, 13–14
    marking, 57
CMOS (Complementary Metal Oxide Semiconductor), 55
    information on, 59, 129
    skipping test of, 100
color, 5
    of box, 3
    modes for, 107
    of prompts, 2
    of window, 6
COMMAND.COM file, 38
command-line help, xiii
Compare Windows option, 26
conditional branching, 2
CONFIG.SYS file, 130
    ANSI.SYS in, 88
    COUNTRY parameter in, 89
    DISKREET in, 41, 45
    editing, 156–157
    NCACHE in, 83
    RAM disk driver in, 53
configuration
    of DISKEDIT, 30–31
    of NDD (Norton Disk Doctor II), 99–100
    of NORTON utilities shell, 106–107
    of SPEEDISK, 119
    of WIPEINFO, 147–148
context-sensitive help, xiii
conventional DOS memory, cache in, 84
copying block of data, 11–12
country setting, changing, 89
CPU speed, information on, 130
cursor, xii, 5
    changing size of, 87
custom error message, setting, 99–100

damaged files, reconstruction of, 71
data, searching for, 33
Data Encoding Testing, 8
data fill, 22
data recovery, after formatting, 145–146
database files, fixing, 71–74
data-read errors, 59
date
    in file search, 66

of system, 89–90
date of file, 34–35, 61–62
dBASE files, 71
defective disks, reviving, 59
DEL command (DOS), 148
DELAY command (BE), 4
Delete key, xii
deleted files, unerasure of, 77
deletion
  of directories, 96
  of NDisks, 47–48
  secure, 147–151
DES file encryption, 46, 51
device drivers, 129, 157
  ANSI.SYS, 5, 88
  DISKREET.SYS, 41, 45, 53
  for NCACHE, 83
DI (Disk Information) program, 127
dialog box menus, xi
directories
  changing, 95, 133–134
  creating, 96
  deleting, 96
  editing, 11, 14–15
  erased, search for erased files in, 137
  linking to, 23
  order of, on disk, 118, 120–121
  recovering deleted, 133
  renaming, 97
  selecting, 14
  TRASHCAN, 77
  wiping files in, 149
directory tree, printing, 97
disk light, turning on or off, 37
disk maps, 124
Disk Protect command, 38
Disk Test (DT) program, 99
DISKEDIT, 11–36
  configuring, 30–31
  quitting, 35–36
  windows in, 25–28
DISKMON, 37–39
DISKREET, 41–53
  in CONFIG.SYS file, 156–157
  quitting, 50
  start-up options for, 52–53
DISKREET.INI file, 42
disks. *See also* floppy disks; formatting
 disks; hard disks
  bootable, 34, 56, 114
  clearing erased files from, 147–148
  defragmenting, 117–118
  overwriting, 148

placing files at beginning of, 118–119
rescanning with NCD, 98
testing and repairing, 101–103
unformatting, 145–146
viewing information on, 123
DISKTOOL, 55–59
display. *See* screen display
DOS colors, changing, 88
DOS commands
  ASSIGN, 10
  BACKUP, 34
  DEL, 148
  FDISK, 18
  FORMAT, 113, 145
  RECOVER, 57–58
  SUBST, 10
  SYS, 56, 114
DOS error messages, 110
DOS memory, information on, 129
DOS operating system
  ERRORLEVEL code, 2
  temporary exit to, 36
double-density disks, 115
drives, 29, 129
  changing, 95, 134
  listing all files on, 134
  selecting, 14, 24, 119

editing. *See also* DISKEDIT
  disabling, 30–31
  undoing, 24–25
Edit/Object functions (DISKEDIT), 11–25
EGA video display card, 107
End key, xii
environment variable, 155
<EOF> marker, 16
erased files
  clearing from disk, 147
  recovery of, 133–143
  search for text in, 136
expanded memory, cache in, 84
exploding window, 6
extended memory, cache in, 84

FA (File Attributes), 11
Fast proprietary file encryption, 46, 51
Fast Wipe, 148
FAT (file allocation table), 133, 147
  checking, 7
  editing, 11, 15–17
  filling in, 22
  saving, 81
FD (File Date and Time), 11
FDISK command (DOS), 18

file allocation table. *See* FAT
file attributes, 15, 33–34, 61
file encryption, 41–53
file fragments, searching for deleted, 135–136
file list, 134, 142–143
    configuring, 62–63
    printing, 67
    sorting, 137
    static, 124
file protection, 77–78
file size, in file search, 66
FILEFIND, 61–70
FILEFIX, 71–75
files
    adding data to existing, 133
    from BE (Batch Enhancer), 1
    changing date and times of, 61–62
    decrypting, 47
    editing, 17–18
    encrypting, 48–49
    finding, 64–66
    going to specific, 66
    linking to, 23
    order of, on disk, 118, 121–122
    protecting, 77–78
    purging, 79
    reconstruction of damaged, 71
    recovering erased, 77, 133–143
    renaming, 135
    searching for, 64–66
    setting date and time of, 34–35
    unerasing, 138–141
    unmovable, 122
    untagging, 141–142
    viewing, 27–28, 31, 69–70, 142
    wiping, 149
FILESAVE, 77–79
filling data, 22
floppy disks, 9. *See also* formatting disks
    protecting against accidental formatting of, 81
    searching for NDisks on, 50
foreground text, 5
FORMAT command (DOS), 113, 145
formatting disks, 38, 59, 113–114
    data recovery after, 145–146
    defaults for, 114–115
    protection against accidental, 81
FR (Format Recover) program, 145
Full Stroke, 8

GOTO command (BE), 4
Government Wipe, 148

graphics options, 107
Grow Window command, 27

hard disks. *See also* formatting disks
    defragmenting/optimizing, 117–118
    interleave for, 7
    parking heads on, 37–39
    speed of, 8, 130
hard-disk controller, checking, 7
hardware interrupts, 129
header of database file, 72–73
help, xiii
Hex converter, 32
hex view, 13, 22
    for file editing, 18
hidden files, 34
    wiping, 149
Home key, xii
hotkey combination, 49

IBMBIO.COM file, 34
IBMDOS.COM file, 34
IDE controller, and CALIBRAT, 9
IMAGE, 81, 114, 145, 155
    help from, xiii
IMAGE.DAT file, 81
Info functions (DISKEDIT), 29–30
information screens, 127
    cycling through, 127
    printing, 128
    viewing, 129–131
installation of Norton Utilities, 153–155
interface, ix–xii, 8
interleave, for hard disk, 7
IO.SYS file, 34

keyboard, repeat rate for, 91–92
keyboard locking, 49
    password and, 42

labels, 1, 4, 96
    for disks, 96
Laptop color mode, 107
linking, 23, 26–27, 31
list boxes, x–xi
Logical drive type, 13, 24
logical sectors, 21
Lotus 1-2-3 files, 71

map, 29–30, 123–124
marking data, 23–24
menus, x–xi, 1
Monochrome mode, 107
mouse, x, 92, 107
moving block of data, 23–24

MSDOS.SYS file, 34

NCACHE program, 83
  help from, xiii
NCC (Norton Control Center), 87–93
NCD (Norton Change Directory), 95–98
NDD (Norton Disk Doctor II), 99–104
  configuring, 99–100
  quitting, 101
  skipping tests in, 100
  undoing changes from, 103
NDisks, 41
  closing , 44–45
  creating, 45–47
  deleting, 47–48
  editing, 48
  opening, 49–50
  password for, 43
  searching floppy disks for, 50
  size adjustment for, 41–42
networks, 129
  drives on, 9
  file search on, 66
  speed of, 130
nondestructive low-level format, 8
Norton Change Directory (NCD), 95–98
Norton Control Center (NCC), 87–93
Norton Disk Doctor II (NDD), 99–104
Norton Integrator (NI), 105
NORTON shell, 105–111
  configuring, 106–107
Novell file servers, 10
NU (Norton Utilities), 11, 133

objects, 25, 29–30
optimization method, for defragmenting
  disks, 119–120
optimum interleave, 8

palette colors, changing, 89
parking hard-disk heads, 37–39
partition tables, 129
  editing, 11, 18–20
  protecting, 38
  skipping tests of, 100
password, 41, 154
  changing, 42
  for file encryption, 49
  for NDisk, 43, 46
Pattern Testing, 8
physical drive type, 13, 24
physical sectors, editing, 20–21
PRINTCHAR command (BE), 4

printing
  directory tree, 97
  file list, 67
  information screens, 128
  system summary report, 127–128
problems, solutions for common, 108–109
program list, 105–106, 108
  sorting, 109
prompts, xii
  customizing, 1
pull-down menus, x

QU (Quick Unerase), 133
Quick Links setting, 31
Quick Move setting, 31
Quit functions (DISKEDIT), 35–36

radio buttons, xi–xii
RAM (random access memory), 7
RAM disks, 9, 53
  file allocation table for, 17
Read Only setting, 30–31
read-only files, 34
  wiping, 149
read/write heads, parking, 37–39
RECOVER command (DOS), 57–58
renaming files, 135
repeat delay, 92
report
  on file fragmentation, 122–123
  on system summary, 127–128
rescue disk, 55–56, 58–59
resizing partitions, 18
resizing windows, 27
root directory, saving, 81
ROWCOL command (BE), 5

SA (Screen Attributes) command (BE), 5
Safe Format (SFORMAT), 113–116, 145
Save IMAGE Info option, 114
screen display
  blanking out, 49
  changing colors on, 87
  changing number of lines on, 95–96
  clearing, 3–4
  writing character to, 4
scroll bar, x
SCSI controller, and CALIBRAT, 9
searching
  for deleted data, 135
  for files, 64–66
  specifying range for, 137–138
  for text, 68–69, 136
sector translation, 9

sectors, 21–22, 24
    editing physical, 20–21
secure deletion, 147–151
security options, 52
Seek Testing, 7–8
serial ports, 90–91
SFORMAT, 113–116, 145
shadow for window, 6
shell. *See* NORTON shell
Shell to DOS command, 36
Shrink Window command, 27
SI (System Information) program, 127
single-sided floppies, 115
slack, 150
software interrupts, information on, 129
Solutions to Common Problems
    function, 99
sorting
    file list, 137
    program list, 109
Speed Search, 95
    for directory, 15
    in SPEEDISK, 123
    in UNERASE, 134
SPEEDISK, 117–125
spreadsheet files, fixing, 74–75
Start and End arrows, 87–88
start-up options
    password and, 42
    setting, 52
static file list, 124
stopwatches, 92–93
subroutines, 1
SUBST command (DOS), 10
surface tests, 99, 102–103, 156
    skipping, 100
Symphony files, 71
SYS command (DOS), 56, 114
SYSINFO, 127–131
    quitting, 128
system configuration, 129
system date and time, changing, 89–90
system files, 34, 38
System Integrity Testing, 7
system memory, 129
system settings, changing, 43–44
system speed, 130
system summary report, 127–128

Tab key, xii
tagging files, for unerasure, 138
Target Fit option, 68
Terminate and Stay Resident programs,
    129
    DISKMON as, 39
    FILESAVE as, 78
text
    attributes of, 100, 105–106
    color of, 88
    searching for, 68–69
time of file, 34–35, 61–62
time of system, 89–90
timeouts
    auto-close, 50–51
    password and, 42
timers, 92–93
toggles, xi–xii
tones, playing, 2
Tools functions (DISKEDIT), 30–35
Track-to-Track, 8
TRASHCAN subdirectory, 77
TREEINFO.NCD file, 98

undoing edits, 24–25
UNERASE, 133–143
UNFORMAT, 145–146
unmovable files, 122, 124
Unsplit Window command
    (DISKEDIT), 25

VDISK, in CONFIG.SYS file, 53
VGA video display card, 107
video card, information on, 129
video mode, changing, 90
views, of files, 27–28, 31
viruses, 38
volume labels, 96, 115

Watches option, 92–93
WINDOW command (BE), 6
Window functions (DISKEDIT), 25–28
Windows 3.0 (Microsoft), 53
WIPEINFO, 147–151
WordStar format, 31
Write To command (DISKEDIT), 25
write-protection, 38

zooming boxes, 107